LARRY L. RASMUSSEN

MORAL FRAGMENTS AND MORAL COMMUNITY

A Proposal for Church in Society

FORTRESS PRESS Minneapolis

MORAL FRAGMENTS AND MORAL COMMUNITY
A Proposal for Church in Society

Cover design: Pollock Design Group
Interior design: The Book Company/Wendy Calmenson

Library of Congress Cataloging-in-Publication data

Rasmussen, Larry L.
Moral fragments and moral community : a proposal for church in society / Larry L. Rasmussen.
p. cm.
Includes bibliographical references and index.
ISBN 0-8006-2757-1 (alk. paper)
1. Sociology, Christian—United States. 2. Christian ethics. 3. United States—Moral conditions. 4. United States—Social conditions—1980– 5. Social ethics. 6. Church and the world. I. Title.
BR526.R365 1993
277.3'0829—dc20 93–18155
CIP

The paper used in this publication meets the minimum requirements of American National Standard for Information Sciences—Permanence of Paper for Printed Library Materials, ANSI Z329.48-1984. ∞™

Manufactured in the U.S.A. 1–2757

97 96 95 94 93 1 2 3 4 5 6 7 8 9 10

The total effect of the rise of a technical civilization and an industrial society has been the destruction of community on the national level and the extension of conflict on the international level.

Reinhold Niebuhr,
The Church and the Disorder of Civilization

Where do we go from here,
chaos or community?

Martin Luther King, Jr.,
Where Do We Go from Here: Chaos or Community?

CONTENTS

Acknowledgments

WRESTLING DOWN A BOOK FROM A LECTURE SERIES REQUIRES MORE than effort and energy. It needs a good occasion and good help. Fortunately I have received both.

The genesis of this book came with the invitation to join Charles Curran for the 1991–92 Hein/Fry Lectures at the seminaries of the Evangelical Lutheran Church in America (ELCA) on the topic, "The Church as a Community of Moral Conviction." That invitation was the work of the Division for Ministry of the ELCA and its director for theological education, Phyllis Anderson. Professor Curran and I each visited four seminaries. I am grateful to Pacific Lutheran Theological Seminary, Lutheran School of Theology at Chicago, Lutheran Theological Southern Seminary, and Lutheran Theological Seminary at Gettysburg for their hospitality, interest, and response.

Yet the lectures were not, it turns out, the book. The more I talked with people and read, the more I stepped back from the topic of the church as a community of moral conviction to the prior and broader question of how communities of character formation are faring in this society, the churches among them. The book begins, then, with a detailed analysis of society and moves from there to the shape and roles of the church. The subject is pretentious—no less than the modern world!—but it is the modern world as focused on the health of those communities whose vocation it is to form moral character and conviction.

This particular outcome was not on the horizon when I received the invitation to give the Hein/Fry Lectures. The book evolved, again with the help of conversations, this time at Union Theological Seminary, New York. Professors Peter Van Ness and Edmund Arens assigned a draft version of the book to the interdisciplinary doctoral seminar. I profited from the classroom discussion, led by Traci West, and from subsequent exchanges. James Martin-Schramm, Elizabeth Bounds, Diane Moore, and Lisa Stoen Hazelwood, all doctoral candidates in Christian ethics at Union, provided separate and detailed response, as did Professor Victoria Erickson, Christian Iosso, and Edward Crane. While the present state of the volume is finally my responsibility, the scholarly collegiality of these friends has left tracks—and improvements—throughout.

Nor dare I forget the anonymous soul, never seen, who faithfully delivers the *New York Times* to our apartment daily at dawn. The footnotes are some measure of my debt to her or him and not a small part of the reason why, at the onset of each day, it seemed compelling to begin serious ecclesial response with equally serious social analysis.

CHAPTER 1

Conclusion and Question

Describing the Moment

"WE ARE LIVING THROUGH A CHANGE OF TIMES," WRITES NOBEL POET and essayist Octavio Paz. We reach for a "rebeginning," "the resurgence of buried realities, the reappearance of what was forgotten and repressed," a return to origins—anything that will lead our weary world to regeneration. "Now that the cruel utopias that bloodied our century have vanished" the time has come "to begin a radical . . . reform of liberal capitalist society" and of the impoverished nations on the periphery.[1] No one can assume that the crisis bringing chaos to countries that lived under the despotism of bureaucratic socialism will not spread to the rest of the world.[2]

Fortunately a saving philosophy may already be riding the wind. Its name is *fraternity* (Paz's gendered synonym for community and solidarity). Fraternity/community/solidarity—the radiant virtue in the sacred triad with liberty and equality all but forgotten in modern democracies, a loss for which we now pay a frightful price. Community, the nexus that "humanizes and harmonizes" the other two, keeps liberty, so prone to abuse, from generating poisonous inequalities, and equality, so inclined to permit tyrannies, from stunting free creativity. Indeed this handsome

[1]Octavio Paz, "Poetry and the Free Market," *The New York Times Book Review*, 8 December 1991, sec. 7, p. 36.
[2]Ibid.

"bridge of interlinked arms" is the "one and only bridge" able to reconcile these contentious siblings.[3] Community saves.

Just in time, for the moment grows grave. Things fly apart. It can even be said, Paz races on, that the main theme of the last days of this century is not the political organization or reorganization of our societies but the question of how humanity is to insure its survival.[4] Yet the kernel of community is there and waits expectantly to crack open with new life.

But not only community, or only community by itself. "The weapon of critical thought" must join it. Community and critical thought, together with "the examination of conscience and the remorse that accompanies it" ("a legacy from Christianity," Paz adds)—*this* ensemble comprises "the most powerful remedy against the ills of our civilization."[5]

Thus says the poet, so free with words, so full of ardor, so ready to read the entrails of modernity, so wonderfully naive about the lurching of history and the ills and cure of civilization!

Whether we share Paz's perspective and exuberance or not, we must begin as he does, analyzing our charged moment in time. Describing deep change while amidst it is formidable, however, something like sketching a bird in flight—Lo, here! Lo, there!—and a few brushstrokes as the swallow disappears from one corner of the horizon only to appear suddenly in another. Nonetheless we must try. The reason is not curiosity alone, or even effective strategy for the church. Faith itself compels it, as the sure echo of God's own ways. For if the incarnation of God is a matter of stipulated time and place ("In the fifteenth year of the reign of Emperor Tiberius, when Pontius Pilate was governor of Judea, and Herod was ruler of Galilee . . . "); and if the way of God is a matter of earthen vessels and spirited flesh ("the word of God came to John son of Zechariah in the wilderness," Luke 3:1–2), then it rests firmly with the faith community to discern the movement of its own incumbent age and fashion living wisdom from the clay of its own appointed earth. Discipleship, Jesus taught, includes watching the sky carefully, discerning the signs and seasons, and investing the age with a feisty hope (Matt. 16:3).

Paz is right, too, that community is the absent subject and the vital center of desperately needed renewal. Whether community can bear his

---

[3]Ibid.
[4]Ibid., 38.
[5]Ibid., 36.

expectant hopes or not, Christians must pay attention to its reality and promise, again for reasons of faith. The originating experience for both Jews and Christians was, it bears remembering, the experience of divine power as the power for peoplehood itself. The God of the biblical communities was none other than the righteous and compassionate One who made of no people a people and hewed a way where there was none. In these traditions community has forever been the nexus of the life of faith and the moral life so vital to it. Moreover it is community of a certain unlikely scope: as near as the neighbor at hand and as boundless as creation itself. When Paz offers community for the care and cure of civilization, or Gar Alperowitz does so to revive exhausted democracy,[6] believers' ears should begin to twitch. *Community* is faith's own vocabulary.

But where is that most venerable institution, the church, now poised? What is its setting and task in this season of extended change? Does it have a judgment about the age and community to offer it? What are its moral resources and its capacity to act redemptively?

The analysis presented here will claim that we careen along the uncertain arch that bridges the modern world and the postmodern. Before the precise contours and meanings are discussed, however, it is important to state the conclusion and set the question.

Conclusion: Our society (the United States) currently lives from moral fragments and community fragments only, and both are being destroyed faster than they are being replenished. This bodes trouble for basic moral formation and community, not to say for society at large. Ours is a season of moral sprawl and breakdown, moral homelessness and drift. Paz may be wholly correct that nothing is so important to civic existence as the regeneration that moral community might provide. It is also, he well knows, inordinately difficult.

Such is the conclusion. Question: Given the claims of Christian faith, and given the requirements of moral formation in a society like ours, indeed a world like ours, what is the shape proper to the church? What are its contributions as a community of moral conviction?

If neither the conclusion nor the question piques the reader's interests or worries, what follows certainly will not. The reader will then have some unexpected free time. The reader might do a pulse check to see whether he or she is among the quick rather than the dead.

---

[6]Gar Alperowitz, "Building a Saving Democracy," *Sojourners* 19 (July 1990): 10–23.

The Church and Moral Criticism

A MORAL ANALYSIS OF MODERNITY AND OUR SOCIETY IS THE HEART OF the first extended segment of this book. It is postponed, however, until we become familiar with key terms of the church as a community of moral conviction. Once oriented to the furnishings of that topic, we can step outside for closely related analysis. Circling the main topic will in fact lead into the analysis of modernity and contemporary American society.

We begin with conscience and convictions. Formed conscience plays out as moral conviction. Granted, some kinds of convictions don't require conscience. We may, for example, be strongly convinced that Pavarotti edges out Domingo and Carreras in the tenor wars and that Wendy's, the clear underdog, is the winner in the burger fray. But it is not possible to have *moral* convictions without conscience, convictions about what is right, good, and fitting from a moral point of view.

We may assume also that conscience and conviction are a matter of community. The word *conscience* comes from *con-sciere*, "to know together." Conscience is the ethical compass of character, and character is formed in community, as moral convictions themselves are. Habits of the heart and habits of moral reflection and decision are possible only as personal expressions of life lived in the presence of one another, with all the blessings and burdens thereof. Community, whether in strong or weak forms, is the matrix of the moral life itself. So if we are able to live with thousands of total strangers at all, that is, live in modern society, it is only by way of what we have learned in the more circumscribed terrain of intimacy, among those who heard our borning cry, who heard our dying one, and who accompanied us on the wondrous and difficult adventure between. "Community and commitments, and the trials thereof," Richard Rohr says, "grow people up."[7] No community, no moral life; no moral life, no society worth living in—it is as simple and basic as that.

Yet this is not to say much. We do not yet know the substance of moral conviction or the character and health of the assumed community. *Community* itself may be both the most popular and the vaguest word in ethics, theology, sociology, and common conversation today. While Robert Nisbet says "community" is the "most fundamental and far-

[7]Richard Rohr, "Why Does Psychology Always Win?" *Sojourners* 20 (November 1991): 14.

reaching of sociology's unit-ideas,"[8] the only common factor in the ninety-four definitions George Hillery, Jr., collected was the unforgiving presence of *homo sapiens*![9] We might well agree with Michael Walzer that "the primary good that we distribute to one another is membership in some human community" and that "men and women without membership anywhere are stateless persons,"[10] just as we might nod in knowing assent as Martin Buber is read aloud in weighty tones: "The primary aspiration of all history is a genuine community of human beings."[11] Yet we are invariably at a loss to specify what "genuine" in "genuine community" genuinely means! Or what community membership as "the primary good" is humanly about.

Moreover, even human beings no longer monopolize community. We are rapidly (or is it very, very slowly?) learning that we must respect biotic networks and ecosystems as genuine communities of life, or we do ourselves in. Already nebulous boundaries thus mist over. *Homo sapiens* are not, it turns out, the only extant citizens of living communities or the only subjects in the moral universe.[12] Do other animals have rights? Do trees have standing? But even for peopled community alone, the interminable chatter on too many slick talk-shows and in too many slick magazines winds down to no more than a certain terminal wistfulness *about* community. In the absence of the real thing, the talk shows themselves become substitute communities, just as televangelism steps in for church and welcome-home parties for returning soldiers supply community for otherwise anonymous suburban neighborhoods. Or, to recall a horrific example, Hitler's blood-and-soil community of magnetic and mystical force surged in a nation's soul, overwhelmed the remnants of more modest and humane communities, and in a few short years created a feverishly patriotic and violent community of the Fatherland.

---

[8]Robert A. Nisbet, *The Sociological Tradition* (New York: Basic Books, 1966), 47.

[9]George A. Hillery, Jr., "Definitions of Community: Areas of Agreement," *Rural Sociology* 20 (1955): 118.

[10]Michael Walzer, *Spheres of Justice* (New York: Basic Books, 1983), 31.

[11]Cited by Frank G. Kirkpatrick, *Community: A Trinity of Models* (Washington, D.C.: Georgetown University Press, 1986), 1. Kirkpatrick is quoting from Martin Buber, *Paths in Utopia* (Boston: Beacon Press, 1958), 133.

[12]Even the word *society* is no longer reserved for human beings only. *Webster's New World Dictionary* (second college edition) includes the following among its definitions: "a group of animals or plants living together in a single environment and regarded as constituting a homogeneous unit or entity."

There are sound historical reasons for this state of confusion about community, and for modern people's susceptibility to the appeal of all manner of communities, including authoritarian and violent ones, as we shall see. For the moment we are still chasing the assigned terms.

The designation "church" is often intended as the decisive clue to the missing substance and shape of community. "Church" names the community under consideration and marks it off from other communities. This particular community of moral conviction arises from the impact of Jesus of Nazareth, claims a collection of wildly diverse Hebrew and Greek writings as its canonical Scriptures, considers these Scriptures as formative for the Christian life, and observes ministries of word, sacrament, and witness around the globe in a remarkable display of both ecumenical diversity and continuity over two full millennia.

This is a sizable deposit for the Christian life. Nonetheless the question is still ambiguous when sharpened in the way it must be, namely: Which conscience and convictions, formed by which Christian community in what way, with whom, where, and to what end? The evidence is clear, for example, that many Afrikaners have well-formed consciences, developed with the care and energy of morally serious generations in a morally intense church. For decades Afrikaner defense of apartheid inhaled and exhaled moral sincerity and rock-ribbed moral conviction. Even their opponents have regarded Afrikaners as people of integrity when integrity means, as it commonly does, taking actions consistent with sincerely held moral convictions.

Or, to shift the example closer to home, the public television series "The Civil War" was replete with moving testimony by white soldiers, in Gray ranks and Blue, who bore every burden and paid every price for a cause they held with fast Christian conviction. In moving letters to distant loved ones and in diaries reserved for the keeping of their own souls, they, like their leaders Lincoln and Lee, witnessed nobly to an anchored morality that provided them their moral compass in that tragic and hideous conflict. While those often reluctant, sometimes eager combatants made a militant noise to the Lord in separate battle hymns, they prayed the same Lord's Prayer and sang the same stanzas of "Amazing Grace" around campfires the length and breadth of both South and North. So while designating "the church" as the "community of moral conviction" is important (it always matters which community shapes character, conscience, and conviction), more important in fact is judging the community's concrete moral quality itself. Not to do so is a massive moral failure in its own right, as black South Africans and African Americans have witnessed to time and again for the struggles just cited, as for others.

Differently said, the formation of moral conviction in Christian communities has often been its malformation. Good people who did not know they were not quite as good as they thought have been racist, sexist, elitist, and blithely uncaring about nature or distant neighbors. Conscientious churchgoers have been as susceptible as any other members of the public to interests that opportunistically work the traffic on both sides of the street. "I wrestled all night with my conscience," Swiss historian Jakob Burckhardt is reputed to have announced to friends in the morning, "but I won!" Because we all win in this way, there is no escaping the responsiblity either for carefully forming moral convictions in the first place or for judging the convictions formed. Whatever other tasks the church has as a community of moral conviction, exercising self-criticism and throwing open the windows to hear from the unchurched are among them.

Self-criticism and openness to others' critique should not be an odd or difficult task for a community whose radical gospel is that the ungodly are justified and that one's performance in the moral life does not determine whether God offers or withholds saving grace. Sound performance in the moral life is vitally important but penultimate in the eyes of a free and gracious God who always seems to be turning the tables anyway.

A different example makes a similar point about the need to examine Christian conviction. The ethos of medieval life was clearly "community." It was community in ways many yearn for and intuitively embrace: life in small social groupings; life lived close to the land; and life quite stable, with well-stipulated duties and responsibilities set within a world well defined and understood. Life was also short, sometimes nasty, often brutish, rather poor, and always hierarchically ordered, with an efficiently demarcated ladder extending from peasant to prince to pope and on through the ethereal ranks of heaven right up to the throne and to the Lamb and the unutterable Name above all Names, all in good order and thoroughly shrouded in the kind of mystery befitting a great cosmic chain of being and its omnipotent Creator. Mysterious or not, it was still very clear that the social order was ontologically buttoned to the cosmic order, and this was the Lord's doing.

The social metaphor for human society in this elaborate scheme was a thoroughly organic one. Thomas Aquinas, echoing Paul, knew full well that everything was connected to everything else in community as parts of the body are to the whole. So medieval life was lived out in village, guild, and feudal class, with nothing so prominent as status and social group linked together in a scheme ordained of God. All of it was "Christian community" and all of it was soaked in Christian culture as everywhere reflected in art, music, manners, trades, titles, literature, and liturgy. It was also ghettoes for the Jews and pograms against them, crusades to battle the infidels with death the punishment of choice, a world of demon exorcisms, the Inquisition and torture, rampant underground spiritualities, subversive mysticisms, and witch and faggot burnings. Would you then, if you could be a pirate of time, choose life in medieval Europe because it was suffused with established Christian community and pervasive Christian morality? Even to hesitate before the answer is to underscore the point: It is not enough simply to favor "living in community," even Christian community. The specific moral character of the community must be judged.

The point must be elaborated for moral convictions in particular. Unshakable belief is not the same as truth, not even when it is the community's truth and not even when it is zealously guarded with the unfailing dedication of true patriots. To say "It doesn't matter what you believe, as long as you're sincere" is to grant permission to Nazism, for example, among other possibilities. Furthermore even our best convictions, convictions that arise in the high country of compassion and flow with passion into actions, can be terribly wrong as moral judgments. They may discern the will of God sincerely but badly. Or, like the blessing of rain become a flood, they may turn destructive as they gain power in the form of channeled behavior in a complex, unpredictable, and often tragic world. There is simply no escape from judging the moral quality of even the most sincere convictions, just as there is simply no refuge anywhere, least of all in God, from moral discernment, responsibility and accountability. Neither is there any community anywhere that guarantees moral success, much less purity. The flight from discernment, responsibility, and criticism ought not to find a gospel of cheap grace anywhere—not in good intentions, ignorance, the right community, or excellent breeding (claiming Abraham as our father, to recall the word of Jesus in John 8:31-59).

Emphasis on moral judgment and criticism escalates when we speak of religious communities in particular. *Religio* means "a uniting bond." It is a special bond, a tether to the sacred and the divine, that strong link to God which holds fast the precious cargo of abiding meaning. With this escalation to levels of ultimate concern, moral convictions will be sheltered by a sacred canopy that does not lightly abide the busy nostrils of critics. Furthermore these moral convictions, because they are wrapped around what matters most in life, always flirt with absolutism and fanaticism. You want to think twice, then, before you recommend the church, or any other communities of fundamental religious intensity, as the communities of moral conviction for society. Religious passion is often the most volatile kind, and most deadly; it is matched only by moral convictions held with religious fervor. Yes, we will have them, willy-nilly, since religion, despite the wishes of its cultured despisers, is not about to lose its color or go out with the tide. It will not do so as long as we are the curious species we have been ever since that first warm night eons ago when the first baby was lifted on strong arms toward the full moon in the awesome presence of waiting gods. The point is simply that criticism of moral convictions and their communities is an enduring task, and communities of religious intensity need vigilant critique as much as any, even when they do not rush to spread the welcome mat. In a word, you should not favor the church as a community of moral conviction if it is not simultaneously a community of moral deliberation and criticism, including self-criticism.

Later we shall speak of the inclusive, or catholic, character of the church as a moral community for our time. Suffice it to say here that moral critique can be institutionalized in two ways. As intimated, one way is to include disparate voices within church ranks. Good hearing—"ears to hear"—and good eyesight—"eyes to see"—are, in part, learned. They are learned as the habit of openness to difference, to revelation, to perspectives and stories other than our most familiar and comforting ones. This habit of welcoming the other includes the capacity to read Scripture itself over against us as a strange and unsettling word. Sound criticism is learned by noticing dissonance and muffled voices and by entertaining questions that unveil incomplete and controversial perceptions. Often the malformed character of a community and its malformed convictions are a downward spiral fed by nothing so much as homogeneity of membership and outlook and unspoken, tight consensus. The community then reads Scripture—and the world—in ways that reinforce its distorted character, and this only undergirds its most oppressive exegesis and moral convictions. That, to recall earlier examples, is exactly what happened in the Dutch Reformed Church in South Africa and in the use of the Bible to justify slavery, racial segregation, and racism itself in the United States.

The other way to institutionalize moral critique and thus submit conviction to ongoing reformation is to learn from those who dwell well beyond church borders. A genuinely catholic church does counter narrow grounds of moral perspective and authority. Yet the danger remains that the community will be subject to that distorted perception which is based in shared interests, in the commonality of mind and outlook that arises even among a diverse membership, and in the strong sense of belonging that forges community in the first place. The making of tragedy is here, since people will accept all manner of foolishness and commit all manner of crimes rather than violate the identity they regard as sacred to their very being. Against this little can be done among voluntary communities, at least from within and noncoercively, except to foster an identity that makes the habit of talking with outsiders and welcoming the stranger part of the community's own life skills. The word from the world (which, we are all reminded, is God's) is often a correcting and teaching word, a revelatory and sometimes saving one. We have it on no less than biblical grounds that not only is dignity accorded the outsider but the stranger is often the designated messenger of God, and a leader of the enemy may even be God's appointed messiah (Cyrus comes to mind). In any case, it is wise to remember that while reality is always many-sided, any single judgment of it can be a partial truth only. "None of us is as smart as all of us" holds for the moral life, as elsewhere.

It is also wise to recall that creation as a whole has primary theological legitimacy. The whole of the human and nonhuman world, and beyond it the reaches of space, is required for the full disclosure of the God we see crystallized in Jesus of Nazareth. The church's legitimacy resides solely in its nature as a servant and friend of God's irrepressible hopes and struggles for a grander community, the awesome cosmos itself.

Perhaps this plea for a wide space for the world and for a critical posture is largely unnecessary, given the current ethos. The ranks of critics, loving and otherwise, are legion today. Perhaps more critics are not required, only able listeners on every side. Yet the call is not for criticism per se but critical analysis that includes many voices. Many voices should always characterize moral and theological discernment, not only for critical analysis as assessment or judgment but for analysis as basic understanding. The world is a dynamic reality, and no given situation is self-interpreting. What the church's world is and how the faith community understands itself in its world always need to be made clear. Clarity about that world is thus a standing element of its moral work together. It matters immensely, then, whether the time of moral decision is the first century, the tenth, sixteenth, or late twentieth; whether the church's social location is New York City, Wyoming, Madras, the Ukraine, the Amazon, or Malawi; whether the community's members are dirt poor, filthy rich, both, or neither; whether the membership is young or old and has lived with the same ZIP code for years or is the terminally transcient; and within the same ZIP code, whether the local culture is Fifth Avenue below Ninety-sixth Street or above it. And, for all of these, who is included in the task of discernment and who is not. The substance of moral conviction and community character are always linked to identities forged in the faith community's own concrete, lived world.

The work of discernment loops back to Octavio Paz's anguish about the current state of the moral life. When we think of the church as a community of moral conviction, we cannot remain silent about time and place. Which church where? What moral convictions directed to whom? Whose blood flows here anyway? Whose noses are pressed against the glass? What horizon connects earth to sky? If any flowers bloom, which?

CHAPTER 2

Modernity and Middle America

Approaches

WHAT IS THE MORAL STATE OF THE UNION? WHAT IS THE MORAL STATE of the culture this book most has in mind—modern U.S. society? The specific social world in view here is the one that has most determined dominant U.S. culture, the one most at home in it, for better and for worse. It is also the dominant culture in the churches to which many readers belong, a culture focused on family, work, education, and a middle-class standard of living.

We might have analyzed modernity from the point of view of its whiteness, its male-mindedness, its class character, or its treatment of nature. All these are below the surface and between the lines. But the presentation here is of history and culture, not in order to escape the strong imprint of race, gender, class, and cosmology but to emphasize their comprehensive nature. That comprehensive nature is itself a coherent culture, one that over a long, wide history has impacted and colonized far beyond the ranks of its progenitors and beneficiaries.

The culture in view—modernity in the United States—spans the range of interests and viewpoints that make ours a modern liberal society. It includes the sway of an open marketplace and capitalist economics, whether laissez-faire or state regulated; it means the presence of a championed individualism that breaks with most traditional communities and inherited restraints; and it lives by a spirit of calculation and pragmatism expressive of personal and collective interests. Both "conservative liberals" and "liberal liberals" are therefore included,[1] that is, both Republicans and Democrats of various overlapping camps. In the churches the span includes what Charles Curran, citing Martin Marty, refers to as "the public church"—Catholics, Orthodox, and mainline and evangelical Protestants, who, while they have separate ecclesial traditions and many internal differences, share a common concern for the public order and the issues and problems of U.S. society.[2] They share a common worry about society and a common sense of responsibility for its welfare as a viable, pluralistic gathering.

The analysis here, to speak in the first person, is offered by a full-fledged, card-carrying member of this society and church who suffers more than a little bourgeois angst about its future. I believe there are, in modernity's life in this society, fragments of redemption attached to the fragments of community and morality. But they are diminishing. More bluntly stated, my conviction is that modernity, for all its splendid achievements, is killing us. It slowly devours its own children as well as the children of others. Such is the perspective, from a point somewhere near the center of this culture itself, that drives the following appraisal of U.S. society.

Where do we begin the analysis? To attempt a full moral State of the Union is wildly pretentious. Even to focus on some small but representative circle of middle America is grandiose.

One possible tack is to visit an important, select social sector and ask about its health. Child rearing and family life jump to mind.

It is moving to hear what led Christopher Lasch to undertake elements of his massive study of modernity, specifically the volumes, *Haven in a Heartless World: The Family Besieged* and *The True and Only Heaven:*

---

[1]The labels are those of Robert Bellah, used to span the range of citizens he and his colleagues investigated in *Habits of the Heart* and *The Good Society*. Which is to say preponderantly middle-class white U.S. Americans heavily invested in the institutions and patterns of modernity as understood in this and subsequent chapters here. I do not know whether Bellah has used these terms in publication. My citation is from his discussions at the conference on *The Good Society* held at the University of California in Berkeley, 9–10 November 1991.

[2]See the discussion in the first chapter of Charles Curran's book *The Church and Morality* and his reference to Marty. "The public church" includes members of the Orthodox communions in the U.S. They are not simply churches of immigrants any longer but of established generations of U.S. citizens.

Progress and Its Critics. As for many of us, his motivations were anguished personal ones, even though the published style more closely resembles the beady-eyed investigation of a distant, circling eagle. By their own testimony, the Lasches "tried to re-create in the circle of our friends the intensity of a common purpose, which could no longer be found in politics or the workplace."[3] The desire was to give "our children" a chance "to grow up in a kind of extended family."[4] In short, the quest was for community.

> A house full of people; a crowded table ranging across the generations; four-hand music at the piano; nonstop conversation and cooking; baseball games and swimming in the afternoon; long walks after dinner; a poker game or Diplomacy or charades in the evening, all these activities mixing children and adults—that was our idea of a well-ordered household and more specifically of a well-ordered education. We had no great confidence in the schools; we knew that if our children were to acquire any of the things we set store by—joy in learning, eagerness for experience, the capacity for love and friendship—they would have to learn the better part of it at home. For that very reason, however, home was not to be thought of simply as the "nuclear family." Its hospitality would have to extend far and wide, stretching its emotional resources to the limit.[5]

The Lasches were moved to this reconfiguration of family and this effort at community by the "unexpectedly rigorous business of bringing up children" in a society that claimed it was "child-centered" but that was in fact icily indifferent "to everything that makes it possible for children to flourish and to grow up to be responsible adults."[6] They felt compelled to take a sober look at the health of this society from a parent's

---

[3]Christopher Lasch, *The True and Only Heaven: Progress and Its Critics* (New York: W. W. Norton, 1991), 32.

[4]Ibid.

[5]Ibid.

[6]Ibid. See the frightening report by Jane Gross, "Collapse of Inner-City Families Creates America's New Orphans," in *New York Times*, 29 March 1992, A1. The percentage of children living in households not headed by a parent was 6.7 percent in 1970, 8.3 percent in 1980, and 9.7 percent in 1990.

point of view. Whether we agree with the full bill of particulars or not, the testimony has resonance.

> To see the modern world from the point of view of a parent is to see it in the worst possible light. This perspective unmistakably reveals the unwholesomeness, not to put it more strongly, of our way of life; our obsession with sex, violence, and the pornography of "making it"; our addictive dependence on drugs, "entertainment," and the evening news; our impatience with anything that limits our sovereign freedom of choice, especially with the constraints of marital and familial ties; our preference for "nonbinding commitments"; our third-rate educational system; our third-rate morality; our refusal to draw a distinction between right and wrong, lest we "impose" our morality on others and thus invite others to "impose" their morality on us; our reluctance to judge or be judged; our indifference to the needs of future generations, as evidenced by our willingness to saddle them with a huge national debt, an overgrown arsenal of destruction, and a deteriorating environment; our inhospitable attitude to the newcomers born into our midst; our unstated assumption, which underlies so much of the propaganda for unlimited abortion, that only those children born for success ought to be allowed to be born at all.[7]

After surveying responses to "the family issue" in government in the 1970s and 1980s, Lasch draws his conclusion: "None of [the] proposals addressed the moral collapse that troubled so many people."[8]

In passing let it be said that most people want a firmly grounded moral life in a world that adds up and aids and abets their survival and interests. They will support fundamentalism, the Social Gospel, or Ethical Culture; revolutionary politics or reactionary ones; one family and community form or another; segregation or multiculturalism; Republican, Democratic, or Independent candidates; New Age mysticism, Goddess or Greek Orthodox spirituality—all or none of the above (but then something else) if they offer moral security, meaning, and order in an

---

[7]Lasch, *The True and Only Heaven*, 33–34.
[8]Ibid., 34.

often capricious world. What most people will not tolerate for long is moral relativism in a world that isn't making any sense and is militating against their welfare. Of course we do experience moral collapse and moral homelessness, just as we experience spiritual drought and bone-crushing weariness. But we normally refuse to let the experience itself become the reigning condition. Indeed if there is no moral security and no sensible cosmos available, we will conjure them up and inflict them on our neighbors. We insist on a faith, a dense moral culture, and some kind of community as "home."

This insistence on moral security and community is often destabilizing. When people find social, political, and economic arrangements violating the conditions for their own secure well-being, they will find ways to resist as best they can, as they will when inherited traditions and arrangements no longer meet new circumstances. This renders society inherently unstable and conflicted, albeit in highly varied degree. Moral conflict is thus a standing characteristic of society, as is political, religious, and other conflict. Much of it may be muted, repressed, or internalized. It is nonetheless real. That the source of this conflict is the quest for moral and religious security is perhaps ironic. But it is not a surprise. One way or another we push for supportive community and a moral universe hospitable to us.

This aside noted, we return to possible approaches for moral analysis. The moral temper in the U.S. can be uncovered in a second way. Instead of a social sector such as the family we can trace a theme that cuts clean across the social order from left to right, top to bottom. The reality of crime, fear, and violence haunts most everyone, of whatever social status or station.

The reality of two hundred million guns in the U.S.,[9] or the Labor Department statistic that there are now more private security guards than members of municipal police forces, could be explored. So could the statistic that the number of prisoners bused into Los Angeles County jails on a daily basis in 1990—2,100—was just a few more than the number of passengers arriving in Los Angeles every day on Greyhound—2,070; or

[9]See the series in the *New York Times*, "200 Million Guns." The last article in the series, by Erik Eckholm, includes extensive statistics about the prevalence and use of firearms in the U.S. as compared with nine other countries. The U.S. ranks highest in the percentages of households with firearms (48.9 percent), in homicides with guns per million people (44.6), and in suicides with guns per million people (73.0). See "Thorny Issue in Gun Control: Curbing Responsible Owners," *New York Times*, 3 April 1992, A1.

the statistic that more people were let out of California jails in 1989 than were graduated from the state's famous, and huge, university system.[10]

It is not only from the Golden State that the sheen of the good life is gone. In 1990 that other mythical definer of the American dream, Texas, reported that for the first time gun deaths surpassed auto fatalities, 3,443 to 3,309. The totals for the last six years combined still favor death by car to death by bullet, however—21,096 to 19,184.[11]

Or consider the 1990 government survey that found that one in five American high school students, and almost one in three boys, sometimes carries a gun, a knife, or another weapon with the stated intent to use it if necessary. The Federal Centers for Disease Control, which made this survey public, had earlier reported that half of high school students drink, that one in three smokes, and, alarmingly, that one in four has seriously considered suicide. In the most recent release, among the students who were armed, 55 percent carried knives and razors, 24 percent clubs, and 21 percent guns. The survey covered more than eleven thousand students in all fifty states, the District of Columbia, and the territories. It was acknowledged that some students who said they carried weapons might have been lying, as a matter of boasting, joking, or some other expression of standard teenage bravado. On the other hand, researchers commented that an even larger number who carry weapons, especially guns, probably would not admit to doing so, even on a questionnaire that did not ask their identity. The figures would then underestimate.[12] In any event, a major study covering statistics from sixteen thousand law enforcement agencies across the U.S. records a 25 percent increase in violent crime by youth over the past decade.[13]

With these statistics in mind, we may or may not agree with Cornel West that

> the most striking feature of contemporary American society is its sheer violence and brutality. Civic terrorism pervades the streets

---

[10]"Why the Sheen Is Gone from the Golden State," *San Jose Mercury News*, 10 November 1991, 20A.

[11]"1990 Gun Deaths Top Auto Fatalities in Texas," *New York Times*, 9 November 1991, L10.

[12]"Twenty Percent in High Schools Found to Carry Weapons," *New York Times*, 11 October 1991, A13.

[13]"Violent Crime by Youth Is Up 25% in 10 Years," *New York Times*, 30 August 1992, A1.

> of our cities. Sexual violation and abuse are commonplace in our personal relationships. And many of our urban schools have become policed combat zones. By the year 2000, much of America may become uninhabitable—that is, it may be impossible to live here without daily fear for one's life,[14]

or with West's contention that "we are the only modern peoples who regard a gun culture as a precondition of liberty."[15] The reader may or may not agree with the National Rifle Association, the Willie Horton White House, the majority of Congress, and perhaps a majority of U.S. citizens that bearing arms is a litmus test of freedom, a matter of fundamental protection, and the correct rendering of the Constitution. The salient point does not rest with agreement or disagreement but with the recognition that the ready recourse to arms in high schools and homes, the levels of fear in many neighborhoods, and the widespread domestic violence across all races and classes, in town, country, city, and suburb signify community decay, moral venom, and the precariousness of those personal bonds of trust and social adhesion on which every healthy society depends. After all, our weapons are almost never gathered, as in some societies, for organized attack on the seats of power. They are not for insurrection. They are reserved for fellow citizens.[16]

Attention to a vital social sector (the family) or an issue crisscrossing society (violence) can serve as the thread to follow in order to see where social morality is intact and where it is unraveling. More helpful, however, is to locate ourselves, like Paz, in the broad sweep of history and from there take the measure of our moment in time.

Modernity Considered

WE ARE POISED, AS SAID AT THE OUTSET, BETWEEN THE MODERN WORLD and the postmodern. Modernity is a canvas of many hues and the subject of a full rain forest of analyses. Thus it is imperative to define its meaning as it is used in these pages: Modernity here is the name for the promise of rational, science-based progress as a human historical project linked to

---

[14]Cornel West, *Prophetic Fragments* (Grand Rapids, Mich.: Wm. B. Eerdmans; Trenton: Africa World Press, 1988), 157.
[15]Ibid.
[16]Ibid.

capitalist and socialist economic engines, with a claim on democracy as the polity of choice, with the nation-state as the primary form of political sovereignty, and with the bourgeoisie as modernity's most prominent inventor as well as its vanguard and heart.

Modernity has global reach now, but it is Western in its origins. Initially it was a reaction against the interminable religious wars that followed the Reformation and the superstition, ignorance, and misery that haunted the Middle Ages. To be sure, sturdy continuities tie modernity's project of a rational order for society, nature, and even psyche to its anchor in the firm medieval conviction that a logical order buoys up the universe itself and holds all things together as harmoniously and securely as the architecture of a cathedral.

But it was with the genuinely epochal break of the Enlightenment of the eighteenth century, the bourgeois revolutions of the same century and the Industrial Revolution and scientific breakthroughs of the eighteenth and nineteenth centuries, that the modern vision itself came into focus. It was a human-centered liberation vision with an optimistic and popular liberation philosophy. "The Enlightenment was the original liberation movement of our time,"[17] writes Albert Borgmann, and what it promised, through science, technology, and a dynamic new economy, was "to bring the forces of nature and culture under control, liberate us from misery and toil and enrich our lives."[18] Finally, after millennia of fitful performance, the power and the pattern for the transformation of human existence and the world came to reside firmly in human hands. Life was no longer fated.

But far more than that, through scientific knowledge and technology, and the extension of industrial civilization and democratic process, poverty, disease, and toil could be supplanted with an abundance that would permit the good life as one of enriching, individual choice in the context of enhanced liberty and untrammeled opportunity. The secularizing of society—a reaction to those religious wars and the heavy hand of the medieval church—and the empowering of humanity would leave us all as the unbounded rulers of ourselves and the earth.[19] Religion, the an-

[17]Albert Borgmann, *Technology and the Character of Contemporary Life: A Philosophical Inquiry* (Chicago: University of Chicago Press, 1984), 35.
[18]Ibid., 41.
[19]The use of *we* and *us* must be noted carefully in the text. I cannot stipulate, with each use, who is included and who is not. In this portrayal of modernity the ref-

cient integrator that underpinned a society's morality, was no longer organizationally necessary for a humane social order and could take its proper, more restricted place as voluntary personal choice and practice.[20] Capitalist economics would offer freedom from economics in the sense that the age-old struggle against scarcity need no longer be a daily human obsession. Democracy would release us from politics as the worry that comes with power in the hands of others not accountable to us. (Democracy responded to the medieval conviction that "error has no rights" by institutionalizing tolerance and a search for truth as the give-and-take of free exchange. This was to break the authoritarianism that concluded that "one Lord, one faith, and one baptism" meant "one king," "one truth," and one "way of life.")

Science-based progress would perhaps contribute most. Since science provided the constant revisioning of things in keeping with tested and self-correcting procedures, it would save us from the terror of change and the paralyzing fear of the unknown. Discontinuity and change, those horrors premodernity imaged in much the same way biblical writers pictured chaos, were now in fact welcomed as the form of indeterminate possibilities.

---

erence is in the first instance to the bourgeoisie, i.e., the "inventors" of modernity and its exuberant champions. But their claims were unabashedly universal, very often naively so. They felt the civilization they were creating was appropriate as the dominant culture for the world. It is clear that not all were included, however, and many were not even welcomed. Hence the present "hermeneutic of suspicion" whenever universalist claims are uttered. This is a hermeneutic grounded in the direct experience of the excluded. My reason for using an unqualified *we* in these pages is to convey the "liberation vision" in the manner its adherents themselves did; thus the text is written in a historically descriptive manner. For other notes on the perspective taken in this chapter, see the discussion at its beginning.

[20]This is not the occasion to discuss the pilgrimage of religion and the rather "exceptional" place it holds in the modern world, beyond noting that modern religion is exceptional in its relegation to the margins of ordinary existence. The longer human tale finds religion as consciously central to survival, morality, and meaning, with social institutions and common rituals making this manifest. It would be a worthy historical study to see how often atheism or some other "free-from-religion" view has been considered an intellectually reasonable and existentially authentic one. Modernity, especially European modernity, has seen this exceptional development.

With such vision and promise as this, it was small wonder that the most youthful nation of modernity, the United States, fresh from its own bourgeois revolution, put *novus ordo seclorum* (new world order) on each dollar bill. Or that apostles of the new age like Francis Bacon wrote volumes titled *Novum Organum* and *The New Atlantis*. They claimed, as Bacon did, that the power of the citizens of a country to subject fellow citizens, and the power of some countries to subject other countries, was crass and vulgar compared with the supreme human vocation itself—the endeavor "to establish and extend the power and dominion of the human race itself over the universe."[21] Evidently we must subjugate something, Langdon Winner comments wryly, and nature and the universe, unlike human beings, will not mind subjugation.[22] Modernity, whose master plan was the plan of mastery itself, had a charged, even fevered, sense of its vocation of progress and control. Its liberation vision burned as confidently as any star in the heavens.

Even the most articulate, penetrating, and organized criticisms of industrial capitalism, the socialist ones, never abandoned the immaculate confidence in scientific technology or the root conviction of the busy bourgeoisie that we could have a world of our own making and it could be good. They claimed only to fulfill modernity's promise of abundance in a far more just and democratic way. In slightly different words, Charlene Spretnak's, modernity had "stripped down the meaning of life to a struggle between the human mind and the rest of the natural world" and, through economic expansion and heightened human agency everywhere, promised "autonomy and deliverance."[23] Thomas McCollough quips that with the triumph of modernity the hard choices of social ethics itself were assumed to be "unnecessary" (continuing technological and socioeconomic advancement would lift all boats), "impossible" (because

---

[21]Francis Bacon, *Novum Organum*, in *Selected Writings*, ed. Hugh G. Dick (New York: Modern Library, 1955), 499. In *Instauratio Magna* he announced his mission: "I am laboring to lay the foundation not of any sect or doctrine, but of human utility and power." Cited from Thomas McCollough, *The Moral Imagination and Public Life: Raising the Political Questions* (Chatham, N.J.: Chatham House Publishers, 1991), 32.

[22]Langdon Winner, *Autonomous Technology* (Cambridge, Mass., and London: MIT Press, 1977), 23.

[23]Charlene Spretnak, *States of Grace: The Recovery of Meaning in the Postmodern Age* (San Francisco: HarperCollins, 1991), 12.

modernity meant the loss of a common religious and moral worldview), and "undesirable" (because of the dangers of imposing a particular morality on a pluralistic society).[24]

Aye, but things go oft awry! The grand promise of modernity—autonomy and deliverance in the blessed form of ever-increasing well-being for all—has foundered, even crashed. Though it has millions of desperate believers still, and for lack of institutional alternatives continues its deadly habits, it bleeds now like the Exxon Valdez or lies beached like some great whale, huge and impressive. More precisely, it remains powerful and active though badly hurt, like a wounded giant floundering about on a series of realities we have only begun to recognize as interlinked: capitalist and socialist economies so totally out of sync with nature's requirements for regeneration as to quietly threaten ecocide; the destruction of indigenous cultures and peoples; the breakdown of close community and organic traditions; the disintegrative effects for society, psyche, and nature of living out the image of mastery and control as the primary image for humanity itself; the development of weapons of apocalyptic destruction; the mountain of debt incurred by maintaining civilization and paying for its debris, costs far exceeding those needed to build it in the first place; the immiseration of the growing urban poor and the evacuation of many rural areas in the manner of "Appalachias"; the recognition that while different, the forms of oppression of women, many minorities, Third World, and indigenous peoples are linked and arise from forces that oppress land and nature as well; and the onset, amid abundance itself, of frazzled nerves, addiction, stress, rootlessness, chronic fatigue, and depression as serious diseases of a scattered soul and a restless, impoverished spirit.

So we arrive at the end of the modern world, feeling about our liberation a little like King Pyrrhus after the battle of Asculum: "Another such victory and we are undone." Or, if not at the end of modernity—it is far from over—we are at least at the entrance to the emergency room, where we wave vigorously for attention and try to admit a world requiring immediate and extended intensive care.

True, as the beneficiaries of modernity most middle Americans have not yet experienced the full ambulance load of pain that it can deliver and has delivered to some peoples. We do not feel quite like the psalmist, who lamented that God had fed the people with the bread of tears and given

---

[24]McCollough, *The Moral Imagination and Public Life*, 29.

them bowls of tears to drink (Ps. 80:5). We are more like those largest dinosaurs whose brains were so far from their tails that the pain of injury only registered some while later. They went on grazing, unfazed, until the pain from their trailing parts finally traveled the many circuits to the head. Yet the injury does register and we begin to speak hesitantly of what comes next, the postmodern.

Post words—postmodern, post-cold war, post-Christendom—always tell us far more about the world we are leaving than the one we are entering. They identify "this passing age," to use Pauline coin, more precisely than the coming one. But for the moment we can say that postmodernity means a yearning and a search, which issue from a set of internal crises (of spirit, meaning, and moral direction) and a set of external ones (of social structures, policies, and organization). It is a yearning of the spirit that modernity promised to satisfy but manifestly has not, even with periodic bursts of hyperactive affluence—megamalls, theme parks, health clubs, 900 numbers, and yoga lessons packaging serenity on videotape.

It is a search for an alternative that does not destroy the (global) village it wishes to save, a search for a practical wisdom rooted "in ecological sanity and meaningful human participation in the unfolding story of the Earth community and the universe."[25] Even beyond the reach of affluence, across the vastly wider worlds of the poor, ours is a time dogged by a worldwide spiritual quest and a desperate search for viable community and social and political arrangements. At the cusp of the millennium, the world is nothing if not unsettled. Much of the planet is in plain jeopardy.

It must be added that quite another side of postmodernity is its severely protestant mood, its atomizing and relativizing of all authorities. Deconstructionist impulses effectively subvert the many claims of modernity to objectivity and universality but, paradoxically, aid and abet modernity's fragmentation. In a postmodern view all great schemes and systems are socially produced means of some group exercising control over another; that is, all relations are power relations, and suspect. The quest for the good and the true by way of individual access to a universal reason is utterly distrusted as well. Postmodernity, then, while clearly a quest for an alternative to a failing modernity, has exacerbated, rather than healed, modernity's undercutting of community and morality. It has

---

[25]Spretnek, *States of Grace*, 4.

further privatized and relativized value positions even as it tries to escape floundering modernity.

Such is the historical sweep at the widest point of the river. Much more could be said. Some should at least be mentioned.

Against the secularizing and cosmopolitan currents of modernity there now arises anew, in frightening degree, old religious passions, buried ethnic nationalisms, atavistic loyalties, and venomous worship of the tribe. At the same time a promising "reenchantment of the world" is happening, challenging what Max Weber called modernity's "disenchantment"—its leeching of the sacred, the mysterious, and the erotic from the world so that a cosmic community of a million living subjects became little more than a ready collection of user-friendly objects for human beings. Disenchantment was also despiritualization—modernity's deadening of nature and its neglect of soul. Reenchantment promises to resurrect awe and mystery where they had withered and gather together a world known through symbol, ritual, and myth, a world long repressed "in favor of a knowing that really meant controlling."[26] In a time awakening to environmental peril, the world's reenchantment may even tie the collective consciousness of all of us together as a planetary people who have no other home than this mysterious blue gem in space, a Noah's ark of life in the vast, empty reaches.

Or we could say more by drawing the lessons of recent history. We have learned in these years not to claim that the impossible cannot happen. Though Mikhail Gorbachev and F. W. de Klerk may well both be gone by the time this ink dries, itself a sign of the times, the end of the Cold War and the dismantling of legalized apartheid could not have been predicted a decade or two ago. Against the apocalypticists, Reinhold Niebuhr's remark about the continued opportunities that history places before societies, even societies in grave straits, is worth recalling:

> It would be wrong . . . to view the history of the world's cultures and civilizations with an eye only upon their decline. They die in the end; but they also live. Their life is a testimony to the creativity of history, even as their death is a proof of the sin in

[26]Rohr, "Why Does Psychology Always Win?", *Sojourners* 20 (November 1991): 12. Readers will enjoy and learn from Tom F. Driver's *The Magic of Ritual: Our Need for Liberating Rites that Transform Our Lives and Our Communities* (San Francisco: Harper San Francisco, 1991).

> history. . . . For God's judgments are never precipitate and the possibilities of repentance and turning from the evil way are many. According to the degree with which civilizations and cultures accept these possibilities of renewal, they may extend their life indeterminately.[27]

Moving from the testimony of history to the truth of parables, we might welcome the energetic Christian hope that knows of the cycle of death and life, of the proverbial grain of wheat fallen to earth, of the power of unnoticed mustard seeds, of *kairos* moments of judgment, crisis, grace, conversion, and rebirth. Such hope is life defending itself against death and against the death of hope itself. It will not be defeated. It will resist and be reborn.

Yet the immediate task is not to say more about the general condition of modernity or the pitfalls and possibilities that await postmodernity. The investment of middle America in both the promise and problematic of modernity is clear, in any event, and that has been the chief matter for this chapter. The next discussion is the long struggle that has rendered community and its morality so problematic when we need them most. The lines to the church as a community of moral formation and conviction are direct.

---

[27]Reinhold Niebuhr, *The Nature and Destiny of Man* (New York: Charles Scribner's Sons, 1943, 1964), 305–6.

CHAPTER 3

Hard Journey, Uncertain Outcome

Community's Changing Face

THERE IS A HISTORY OF COMMUNITY TO FUSS WITH A WHILE. IT IS FULLY entangled with the history of modernity. The tensions are still with us.

Until our era the notion of community itself was taken utterly for granted. "From the well-known opening sentence of Aristotle's *Politics* to the French constitution of 1958," Carl Friedrich notes, "community has served to designate the human group with which politics and law are concerned and to which all the characteristic phenomena of political life, power, authority, law, and the rest must be referred."[1] Friedrich's reference is to the organic character of society as that had evolved and been lived out chiefly in villages and small towns. Sometimes for better, often for worse, a clear moral order was a standing element of this. Even provincial and imperial cities reflected the moral intactness that was associated with small-scale and more or less settled human community.

Yet Friedrich exaggerates the hold of community in the modern era by a century and more. Part of modernity's experiment was to replace community with the nation-state as the reference point for "all the characteristic phenomena of political life,"[2] a move largely begun with the

[1]Carl J. Friedrich, "The Concept of Community in the History of Political and Legal Philosophy," in *Community*, ed. Carl J. Friedrich (New York: Liberal Arts Press, 1959), 3, as cited by Thomas McCollough, *The Moral Imagination and Public Life: Raising Political Questions* (Chatham, N.J.: Chatham House Publishers, 1991), 71.

[2]Friedrich, "The Concept of Community," 3.

Peace of Westphalia in 1648. In any event,a battle between traditional community and modernity has been quietly waged from modernity's beginnings. The tensions were in fact immediately noted by the very first generation of social theorists a century ago. They made them the subject of their own intense study from the outset. Of that extraordinary cabal, Emile Durkheim was the one who provided the classic diagnosis of modernity's rootlessness, long before we had the vocabulary of "the portable self" in a malleable world on the move.[3] Yet Durkheim also sniffed the heady fragrance of freedom that modernity paraded as its own allure and promise. Persons are "far more free in the midst of a throng than in a small coterie," he wrote, and in an early apology for pluralism he went on to say that the "individual diversities" that modern society encourages put a welcome end to the "collective tyranny" of those closely knit groups that small, static worlds produce with suffocating perfection.[4]

What the sociologists found was that the new economy of the bourgeoisie, with its rationalization, mobility, and transformation of all things into commodities of exchange, destroyed the kinds of intact, long-haul communities that created identity and memory on the basis of community solidarity. Such communities could not withstand the mobility of labor and capital required by the dynamic new economy, nor the fascination with the new worlds it opened to those who would climb aboard. If members of these communities were to get in on the program, they had to move, figuratively and literally. In a word, traditional communities were precapitalist communities, and capitalist economy undercut their stability and values about the same time the nation-state drained off their political significance.

The Protestant Reformation added its own considerable power. It gave an immense boost to the notion of individual moral personhood within society and to the notion of society itself as composed of individuals who carried salvation as well as damnation within their agitated souls. This "introjection of grace within the orders of the world,"[5] when coupled with the breakup of medieval social patterns by the gathering forces of modernity, meant that a *societas* of individuals replaced the Catholic *universitas* of a hierarchically ordered whole. Few notions would better serve the new dy-

[3]This is a reference to a discussion in chapter 5.

[4]Durkheim as cited by Christopher Lasch in *The True and Only Heaven: Progress and Its Critics* (New York: W. W. Norton, 1991), 144.

[5]Adam Seligman, *The Idea of Civil Society* (New York: The Free Press, 1992), 71.

namism than a notion of world-engaged "saints" who stood in unmediated relation to the source of transcendent power and authority.

Often the subsequent destruction of traditional communities—communities whose solidarity was based in kinship, ethnicity, and territorial identity, as well as inherited social standing—was touted as freedom itself, and with some justification. Modernity did rescue many from the tyranny of oppressive and static feudal arrangements, from the small-mindedness of small towns and the insufferable pettiness of village life. To adapt an image from Stephen King in *The Stand*, these were morally stiff communities that had "slapped three coats of lacquer and one of quick-dry cement on [their] way of looking at things and called it good." They all had their own informal security forces who acted like the guards in a local museum of morality, giving anyone tampering with the exhibits "a lot of look-out-below."[6] Given a community ethos like this, millions relished climbing aboard the new adventures. Modernity meant emancipation, freethinking, an open future, and the promise of progress itself. Durkheim, though convinced that some kind of innate social solidarity or *conscience collective* would need to stand in for the social sources of medieval order, understood full well why "you can't keep 'em down on the farm once they have seen Par-ee."

Most of Durkheim's peers—Weber, Freud, Georg Simmel—shared the same ambivalence about the unraveling of secure traditional communities and the ascendancy of the new and heady philosophy of progress. Like him, they affirmed the general direction of the history in which they stood. Like him, they also saw the formation of a set of bourgeois beliefs and sentiments that gave cultural and moral coherence to society (the needed *conscience collective*). But they knew as well that progress came at the steep expense of scuttling those human treasures of identity and security that only settled community provides. Curiously it was Karl Marx among the first-generation greats who considered the reservations about the fragmentation of community, the anomie of urban life, and the subordination of spiritual, contemplative, and cultural energies to the driving ways of the market to be mostly sentimentality. Marx in fact lavishly praised the capitalists for their

---

[6]I am grateful to James M. Childs, Jr., for this image from Stephen King, *The Stand* (New York: NAL Penguin, 1980), 53–54. Childs uses it in his own book on ethics and Christian community: *Faith, Formation, and Decision: Ethics in the Community of Promise* (Minneapolis: Fortress Press, 1991), 19.

ruthless dismantling of feudal society and was convinced that history would honor them for this necessary contribution. That static world needed to be swept into the dustbin of history if human aspirations were to realize the greater possibilities that awaited them. It was simply that modernity's chief value of individual self-realization would not be achieved, he thought, nor the unity of the individual and society accomplished, until capitalism had run its exhilarating but ruinous course and marched with awesome and awful *Sturm und Drang* over into postcapitalist socialism. Thus communism, despite the affinity for "community" in its very name, in its dream for society, and in its list of official values, was even less reticent than capitalism about the wholesale demolition of local communities. Paradoxically, then, the strongest critics of the bourgeoisie's own creation (capitalism as the economic engine of modernity) were even more enamored with aspects of modernity's logic than the bourgeoisie itself!

(Bourgeois doubts about modernity and community would last until "the second bourgeois revolution" of Milton Friedman, Gary Becker, Ronald Reagan, and the United States in the 1970s and 1980s. Thereafter their doubts dissolved, about the time socialist confidence crumbled completely. Modernity's paradox thus runs in reverse, as we shall see.)

The vacuum left by eroding communities was soon noted. John Dewey said with noticeable anguish in 1927: "Our concern at this time is to state how it is that the machine age in developing the Great Society has invaded and partially disintegrated the small communities of former times without generating a Great Community."[7] A Great Community we did not get. What we got was a way of life and style of thinking that regarded persons in largely economic terms; that is, as autonomous creatures who, on the basis of their own wants and preferences, fashion their own world in a series of relationships they themselves make and unmake. This dissolves not only traditional intact communities but a sense for the collective good and public life itself. Public life, reserved largely to males for millennia, had long been understood as the arena of highest human achievement and fulfillment. (The Greek word for "idiot" refers to one who never escapes private life for public experience and service.)

---

[7]John Dewey, *The Public and Its Problems* (1927), in *John Dewey: The Later Works*, ed. Jo Ann Boydston, 2:1925–27 (Carbondale and Edwardsville: Southern Illinois University Press, 1984), 314, as cited in Robert N. Bellah, Richard Madsen, William M. Sullivan, Ann Swidler, and Steven M. Tipton, *The Good Society* (New York: Alfred A. Knopf, 1991), 7.

So while Dewey was in step with the earlier generation of observers in not lamenting the passing of stultifying parochial communities, he warned of the concomitant loss of an essential public identity. The same 1927 volume, *The Public and Its Problems*, continues: "Whatever the future may have in store, one thing is certain. Unless local communal life can be restored, the public cannot adequately resolve its most urgent problem, to find and identify itself."[8] To find and identify itself remains the task, but the communities are largely gone. And absent the moral formation done in local communities, absent the virtues, values, obligations, and identity learned there, there is hardly a vocabulary for public moral discourse, much less the skills needed for pursuing the common good together.

The notion of the common good is itself as thin as the first ice on the pond when the landscape is as barren as it is without "local communal life." What we have now, seven decades after Dewey posted his worry, is the moral sprawl of some scattered community fragments and the remnants of hopes for a Great Community somehow fastened to or built up from restored locales. We also have the remaining defenders of modernity-without-community, individuals for whom liberty and equality, a procedural state, and a vigorous market are conditions sufficient for society. Now, however, more and more people sense that community's loss is also modernity's. Not that this sense was first voiced by Dewey. Two decades before his volume, Max Weber ended a more famous one with the conclusion that the secularized and routinized ways of technical rationality and mass society had denuded the various realms of life of any value, especially ethical value, except the instrumental calculus of means and ends. This "disenchantment of the world" has left us, Weber wrote in 1904, as "specialists without spirit" and "sensualists without heart," who imagine that "this nullity" is "a level of civilization never before achieved."[9] Its most noticeable stamp is "economic compulsion" detached from "the highest spiritual and cultural values."[10] "In the field of its highest development, in the United States, the pursuit of wealth, stripped of its religious and ethical meaning," Weber noted at the turn of the century, "tends to become asso-

[8]Ibid., 370, as cited in Bellah et al., *The Good Society*, 263.
[9]Max Weber, The Protestant Ethic and the Spirit of Capitalism, trans. Talcott Parsons from the 1904 German edition (New York: Charles Scribner's Sons, 1958), 182.
[10]Ibid.

ciated with purely mundane passions, which often actually give it the character of sport."[11]

But this is to run on ahead of the story. We need to look more closely at community's hard journey.

What actually transpired in the course of community's pilgrimage? What hopes guided and animated it? Have we truly landed only in Weber's "iron cage" of "economic compulsion" and Dewey's society-without-community?

With the march of progress underway, swollen as it was with a sense of historical inevitability, at least in the view of its champions, the hope was to combine communal and noncommunal ways so that we could have both "community" and (modern) "society," both *Gemeinschaft* and *Gesellschaft*.[12] Close communitarian ties would provide necessary rootedness, while the looser associational ones of wider worlds would let us move in all the directions required for individual creativity and fulfillment.[13] Modernity's assumption of a basic affinity and fit between individual and community would be proven valid.

The form this partnership took was in fact a drastic change for community, however. In the seventeenth century, community as place and community as experience had been one and the same. But in the great shake-up of the world through industrialism, community and modern society could coexist only if community were no longer a place and a tradition but instead an experience. With the march of modernity, community had to depend less and less on the familiarity of territory and the intimate geography of "home," just as it had to loosen its grip on a well-defined way of life pursued up one generation of the family tree and down the next. Community had to take the form largely of voluntary organizations that could root, spring up, branch out, and be transplanted as need be. It had to demonstrate that it could convene, dissolve, and

---

[11]Ibid.

[12]The reference is to the typology that long dominated the debate over the tensions of community (*Gemeinschaft*) and society (*Gesellschaft*), that of Ferdinand Toennies. See Toennies's *Community and Society*, trans. Charles P. Loomis (New York: Harper & Row, 1963).

[13]One of the classics of the liberal modern tradition is John Stuart Mill's *On Liberty*. Of it Mills says: "The grand, leading principle, towards which every argument unfolded in these pages directly converges, is the absolute and essential importance of human development in its richest diversity." This is from the title page. See the edition edited by Currin V. Shields (Indianapolis, Ind.: Liberal Arts Press, 1956).

begin anew in step with the gait of a fast-paced world. It had to change form from the week in–week out, decade in–decade out gathering of familiar families on the square in front of the cathedral and become instead a traveling road show with an ever-changing cast.

To overstate only slightly: Community had to be transformed from organism to artifact, from a given tradition to a new construct. For many at the time, however, the change seemed like something else. Not the change from organism to artifact, but the thrilling change from one organism—a sluggish caterpiller confined to a small and soggy patch of earth—to another—an elegant butterfly free to make long journeys a little at a time.

With the uprising of the modern world, then, separation occurred between community as place and community as experience. If there was continuity at all, it was community as that blessed company of family, friends, and acquaintances who satisfied the never-dying need for intimacy and belonging, that sanctified church which gathered the emotions and catered the banquet of wisdom needed for whatever struggles the day might deliver. In this way, so it was thought, so it was ardently hoped, and so it also sometimes worked out, community and society could coexist, with good redounding to all. Even misplaced nostalgia for "the vanished warmth of the simple community"[14]—Grandma's fresh-baked bread and mugs of warm milk shared around the stove—need not go wholly unaccommodated, since community would be safely, efficaciously tucked *within* society.

Nor would society need to give up its slow and often bloody extension of franchise, emancipation, and opportunity to more and more members. In the courtship envisioned and now underway, society would comprise the great "systems-world," those grand and necessary arrangements of economy and state, while community would supply the required moral fiber and meet the need for companionship. Moreover, elements of community as experience and as "process" (to use that archetypal modern word) could be grafted onto the main stem of new organizations. This would humanize the world of changing, role-oriented associations and invest assembly line and

---

[14]Sheldon Wolin, *Politics and Visions: Continuity and Innovation in Western Political Thought* (Boston: Little, Brown, 1960), 366, as cited by Thomas Bender, *Community and Social Change in America* (New Brunswick, N.J.: Rutgers University Press, 1978), 143.

office with the ethos of family teamwork and cooperation.[15] Such was the dream and expectation.

Community and Civil Society

REGRETTABLY THIS HOPELESSLY ROMANTIC BUT WELCOMED MARRIAGE, like so many modern marriages, did not work out. Yet it was not for trying! Although from Adam Smith to Reinhold Niebuhr it was assumed that differences of moral temper, even different proximate moralities, existed in public and private spheres, it was nonetheless believed that protected, private communities of intimacy could and would be the civilizing source for the competitive rough-and-tumble of public life. Not a small part of this depended on what Niebuhr referred to as "the superior agape"[16] of women and the warm womb of moral nurture in family, household, and local community. But community was even more, and Adam Smith can be cited to show how it was understood to survive with grace and serve as a moral force within modern society, indeed as the backbone of the indispensable sector often referred to as "civil society." (Civil society is that "space of uncoerced human association" and "the set of relational networks"[17] and institutions that fill it, all trying to harmonize the conflicting demands of individual interests and the social good. Families, schools, churches, synagogues, mosques, voluntary societies, nongovernmental organizations, and communications media all belong to civil society.)

Since we live in the second bourgeois revolution and read the history of capitalism and modern society through it, namely, backward, it is crucial to note first that Adam Smith did not trust the morality of the market as a morality for society at large. He in fact did not even envision a cap-

---

[15]Bender, *Community and Social Change*, discussing Wolin. This grafting has often trivialized community, to be sure, as when the local branch of a far-flung house of investing services welcomes anonymous citizens as "members of the family." As Bender points out, such trivialization, common to our time, makes people more susceptible to the appeal of substitute communities. When these then disappointment them, widespread distrust of institutions occurs and cynicism is created about the possibilities of significant belonging at all.

[16]Reinhold Niebuhr, "From Life's Sidelines," *Christian Century* 101 (19–26 December 1984): 1196.

[17]From Michael Walzer, "The Idea of Civil Society," *Dissent*, Spring 1991, 293.

italist *society*. He envisioned a capitalist *economy* within a society held together by noncapitalist moral sentiments. He and others certainly did consider self-interested actions a virtue for the generation of wealth and self-interested calculations the proper way of making the many decisions of political economy. Against the standing condemnation of insatiable appetites and the vices of envy, pride, and ambition, Smith thought they would assure the never-ending expansion of productive forces in much the same way that the insatiable thirst for knowledge drove the new science and technology.[18] This moral rehabilitation of desire[19] "roused men from their indolence,"[20] said David Hume agreeing with Smith, and led to "further improvements in every branch of domestic as well as foreign trade,"[21] thus effecting new employment and wealth and generally serving society with a rising level of productivity.[22]

But the moral transformation of some private vices into public virtues was warranted only if restricted to the domain of economic exchange. "Economic man" was certainly not the whole "man" but the individual when trundling off to "truck, barter, and exchange."[23] Moreover even "economic man" was driven by a deception, Smith observed, the deception that happiness and fulfillment came with success in the marketplace. Nonetheless it was a socially fruitful deception because it "rouses and keeps in continual motion the industry of mankind."[24] Thus while personal happiness did not trail in the wake of "economic man's" fevered activity—old age would reveal the emptiness of possessions, Smith noted—society as a whole would be well served by it.

The mistake was to let the tawdry dream of commercial success spill over to other relationships; in different words, to let market behavior deter-

---

[18]Lasch, *The True and Only Heaven*, 52.
[19]Ibid.
[20]David Hume as cited by Lasch, ibid., 53. Unfortunately Lasch supplies no footnotes or endnotes for quotations, only a bibliographical essay for each chapter. But even the essay does not list the works of Hume used, much less the specific source of this or other quotations.
[21]Hume, from Lasch, ibid.
[22]Ibid.
[23]Adam Smith, *The Wealth of Nations* (New York: Modern Library, 1937), 14. As cited from Alan Wolfe, *Whose Keeper? Social Science and Moral Obligation* (Berkeley, Los Angeles, London: University of California Press, 1989), 29.
[24]Smith, cited by Lasch, *The True and Only Heaven*, 55. Lasch indicates this is from *The Theory of Moral Sentiments* but does not say where it is found there.

mine culture.[25] In fact familial and other face-to-face relationships associated with friendship and the ways of small towns had the crucial task of domesticating ambition, desire, and the urges of self-indulgence and gratification. In a complicated social ecology, these communitarian relationships would nurture nonmarket civic virtues, which would cultivate social responsibility. The sense of social responsibility in turn would keep the potentially corrupting ways of commerce from poisoning the common good and would in fact channel market energies so as to serve it.

In another twist and turn, Smith understood that nonmarket values were themselves essential for market activity, though market activity did not supply them. Honesty, discipline, deferred gratification, thrift, patience, cooperation, and promise keeping were not learned initially on the job, even though they might be cultivated there. Yet they were as crucial to good business ethos and efficiency as new technologies. In any case, religion and the family especially had the task not only of reigning in the appetites and providing a counterweight to acquisitive individualism but of nursing a whole set of virtues necessary for an orderly moral life amid modernity's dynamic change.

While Smith's stance is clear, a brief discussion of his theory of morality and society is helpful to later discussions.

Smith's first major work, *The Theory of Moral Sentiments*—to his mind the necessary compendium to the more famous *The Wealth of Nations*—opens with his view of the social embeddedness of human nature and the social nature of the moral universe itself. "How selfish soever man may be supposed, there are evidently some principles in his nature, which interest him in the fortunes of others, and render their happiness necessary to him, though he derives nothing from it except the pleasure of seeing it."[26] Evidently we are so constituted that the well-being of others is necessary to our own, including the health of our spirit. The social fabric of mutual welfare isn't a given, however, even when it expresses "some principles in [our] nature." Moral sentiments must be learned, virtues and values must be acquired. Each person, Smith ex-

---

[25]To speak of the market is later lingo, not Smith's. Smith spoke of "markets" but not "the market." This is itself an indication of what is said above, that he really could not envision a capitalist society but only a capitalist economy within society. The use of the phrase "the market" in this context foreshadows things to come, not the apparatus of Smith's own mind and world.

[26]Adam Smith, *The Theory of Moral Sentiments*, ed. D. D. Raphael and A. L. Macfie (Oxford: Clarendon Press, 1976), 9.

plains in an example, should "endeavor, as much as he can, to put himself in the situation of the other, and to bring home to himself every little circumstance of distress which can possibly occur to the sufferer."[27] Thus we learn sympathy through empathy, to illustrate one crucial—and noncapitalist—moral sentiment. A disposition of other-regarding responsibility, itself a requisite of society for Smith, is thereby generated and renewed.

If nurturing noncapitalist moral sentiments is vital, so, too, is protection against their corruption. As Alan Wolfe notes, it is the "great founder of capitalist economics" who says that a "disposition to admire, and almost to worship, the rich and the powerful, and to despise, or, at least, to neglect persons of poor and mean condition, though necessary both to establish and to maintain the distinction of ranks and order in society, is, at the same time, the great and most universal cause of the corruption of our moral sentiments."[28]

In a word, Smith assumed the existence of civil society distinct from a sector organized by economic principles. And he assumed communities of moral formation as indispensable to that society. Civil society even made the ways of economic man possible by securing a moral order within which trucking, bartering, and exchanging could serve the improvement of the material condition of the population. By contrast, exchange motivated by self-interest, however appropriate for economic life, could never sustain the moral relationships of civil society, because it lacked sympathy.[29]

We need not further pursue Smith's understanding of society and the generation of its moral fiber. Important is his assumption—quite erroneous, it turns out—that a symbiotic relationship healthful for both community and society would continue, and that this relationship would take the form of a capitalist economy within society, a society held together by communities of noncapitalist and nonmarket morality. Seligman is correct that this classic picture of civil society as a moral order in which human drives of altruism and mutuality are harmonized with drives of self-interest would not endure "the expansion of capitalism or the growth of rationality,"[30] that the synthesis of community-preserving

---

[27]Ibid., 21 as cited by Wolfe, *Whose Keeper?* 29.
[28]Ibid., 61, in Wolfe, ibid., 29.
[29]Wolfe, ibid., 194.
[30]Seligman, *The Idea of Civil Society*, 31.

action and interest-motivated action in the most dynamic sectors of modernity—the economic and technological—would not "take," and that "a realm of solidarity held together by the force of moral sentiments and natural affections" would not suffice to hold society itself together.[31]

In the end, however, the flaw is deeper. It is the assumption not only of the compatibility of these elements as a moral order, but the assumption that by and large morally competent individuals would populate the public arena and pursue economic exchange, or they would become so (morally competent) in the process. It is an assumption that took the processes of moral formation utterly for granted and badly underestimated their vulnerability to the acids of modernity.

Fast Forward

If a "fast forward" be permitted, we can see what happened over the course of the next two centuries. In Alan Wolfe's words: "Capitalism lived its first hundred years off the precapitalist morality it inherited from traditional religion and social structure."[32] (The reference is to medieval and Reformation Christendom.) Capitalism then proceeded to live its second hundred years "off the moral capital of social democracy"[33] (economic reform movements of the nineteenth and twentieth centuries). Precapitalist moral currents included an emphasis on self-restraint, charity, and an organic sense of society. This was rooted in traditional, that is, precapitalist, communities, and it countered some of the damage unleashed by the acquisitive interests now gaining ground everywhere. Social democracy, which came along about the time the traditional religious, family, and community bonds were weakening, supplied its own moral substance. It fostered a sense of solidarity, a concern to protect the weak and neglected, and a vision of the common good, just as it disciplined private authority with the power of public authority (the state). This took some of the hard edge off the inequalities and neglect that markets generated. To Wolfe's observation should be added that social democracy, too, drew from the moral legacy of traditional communities. Indeed the very rhetoric of social democracy movements was communitarian and even familial. Members freely called one another

---

[31]Ibid., 33.
[32]Wolfe, *Whose Keeper?* 30.
[33]Ibid.

brother and sister and consistently invoked the spirit of collective family struggle and celebration.

The same fast forward would let us see that civil society—that collection of nonmarket, nonstate communities and associations that lets people define who they are culturally and morally through mutuality and reciprocal recognition—would increasingly give way to market and state as the models of society itself and as the chief moral agents of society.

But this races ahead and leaves important episodes behind. We must freeze a couple of frames blurred in the fast forward.

The first frame is the United States a century after Smith. New York minister Henry W. Bellows described what was happening to town life in 1872:

> Thousands of American towns, with an independent life of their own, isolated, trusting to themselves, in need of knowing and honoring native ability and skill in local affairs . . . have been pierced to the heart by the railroad which they helped to build to aggrandize their importance. It has gone through them in a double sense—stringing them like beads on a thread, to hang around the neck of some proud city. It has annihilated their old importance; broken up the dependence of their farmers upon the home traders; . . . destroyed local business and taken out of town the enterprising young men, beside exciting the ambition of those once content with a local importance, to seek larger spheres of life.[34]

A quarter century later social theorist Edward Ross used images reminiscent of Bellows's railroad and the "double sense" in which it tore through the towns. "Powerful forces are more and more transforming *community* into *society*," Ross wrote with unusual precision, "replacing living tissue with structures held together by rivets and screws."[35] The world was on the move, and community ties associated with place were being transformed into transpersonal ones characteristic of business,

---

[34]Henry W. Bellows, "The Townward Tendency," *The City*, 1872, 38, as cited by Bender, *Community and Social Change*, 110. Further publication data not supplied by Bender.

[35]Edward A. Ross, *Social Control: A Survey of the Foundations of Order* (Cleveland: Case Western Reserve University, 1969), 432, as cited by Bender, *Community and Social Change*, 35.

government, mass transportation, mass media, and metropolitan transactions of all kinds.

Yet community, at least as the kind of social relationship that once characterized local and more or less settled communities, would not die, either as the stuff of nostalgia or as the actual character of life in city and country alike. As a social form (voluntary organizations and the family) and as an experience (a sense of meaningful belonging), it refused to collapse even though it was less and less the public face of people's daily life and more and more the place of private moments, a sphere increasingly removed from economic life, governance, even schooling.

(We shall soon see that market and state, rather than local communities, were far more able to coordinate an existence formed and impacted by the interdependence of millions of strangers who shared a common life, albeit in wildly different and unequal ways.)

Jump to the next frame. The rumor of its death premature, community's marriage to society was to be happiest and most harmonious in the new suburbs that sprouted after World War II like mushrooms in a damp forest. They grew in proportion to the choices a dynamic economy permitted to an expanding urban middle class in the 1950s and 1960s. If we had not achieved the Great Community Dewey had hoped for, at least we had the suburb as a desireable stand-in.

The suburb was the modern matchmaker's ultimate accomplishment. It offered not only the very best of the ethos of the communities many suburbanites had migrated from—neighborliness, a zest for voluntary service, a cooperative spirit, trust, altruism—but also the best of modernity itself, the creative flourishing of the individual in the context of a freeing abundance. It offered these treasures of both community and society at a safe remove from the competitive and brutal ways of the market, not to say a safe remove from the hard-edged and dangerous ways of the city. The suburb was modernity's own haven on modernity's own generous terms, complemented with community shorn of its very worst features, the parochial bent of those small worlds and their tight, segregated moralities.

But suburban life, now home to a full half of the U.S. population,[36] has hardly met its promise. This marriage did not quite work out, either. Contemporary suburbanites, as experience testifies and Mark Baldas-

[36]"Those Lights in Big Cities Get Brighter, Census Finds," *New York Times*, 18 December 1991, A24.

sare's studies confirm, tend "to be pessimistic, distrustful, unwilling to tax themselves to pay for services [they demand], and hostile toward newcomers."[37] Moreover drugs, crime, diseases of the spirit, domestic violence, rootlessness, and a chilling anonymity are no longer the monopoly of the cities left behind. Even the triumvirate that most captivates American moral imagination—family, education, and neighborhood community—suffers grave trouble where it was to be most secure, in the suburbs. Even the boast (or complaint) that suburban culture was strong to the point of conformity turns out not to be the case. The suburb is as anomic as the city and nearly as fragile.

The conventional thesis is that the city with its problems has, like some contagion, "spread" to the suburb or, like some alien force, has "invaded" it. The usual response, household income permitting, is to move farther out.

The far likelier explanation of suburban woes is the increasing purchase of modernity's ethos and logic, in particular the extended reach of a market mentality and a democracy run on "interests." It is not that the city has invaded the suburb. Rather both have embraced the second bourgeois revolution.

The second bourgeois revolution has been mentioned but not discussed. Although we need not describe it at length, we do need to map its core logic, since its moral journey is still underway and highly influential.

Key for the second bourgeois revolution is that the moral order and culture are organized on the same principles as the economy and share its ethos. In a development Adam Smith would have found startling, had he been able to conceive it at all, the second revolution denies what the first bourgeois revolution deemed necessary—the existence of noneconomic ties of trust and solidarity fostered by civil society as a related but separate sector. The second revolution says all society and its decisions can be fashioned and executed in the manner economic actors do—with the calculation of self- and group interest in relationships that are fundamentally instrumental in character. Stripped down, the second revolution claims simply that rational self-interest is the one language everyone understands and ought to apply to decisions and actions in every domain. It

---

[37]Wolfe, *Whose Keeper?* 68, drawing from Mark Baldassare, *Trouble in Paradise: The Suburban Transformation in America* (New York: Columbia University Press, 1986), 101–68.

thereby provides a predictable objective order in which all participate on grounds all understand and can affect through the choices they make.

Gary Becker, a Nobel laureate from of the "Chicago School" of economics, represents the second revolution with as little guile as any. He is fully aware that he is arguing against Smith's refusal to extend the logic of self-interest into noneconomic territory, together with Smith's corollary conviction that different spheres require different moralities. Market principles are "applicable to all human behavior," Becker writes against the traditional bourgeoisie, "be it behavior involving money prices or imputed shadow prices, repeated or infrequent decisions, large or minor decisions, emotional or mechanical ends, rich or poor persons, men or women, adults or children, brilliant or stupid persons, patients or therapists, businessmen or politicians, teachers or students."[38] In this scheme individuals are all "utility maximizers" who operate from a relatively stable set of personal preferences. This, Becker says, provides "a valuable unified framework for understanding *all* human behavior"[39] and a framework for all our moral decisions. Quite apart from markets, then, there is a mental process of market behavior and logic that supplies all the guidance needed for moral and other considerations necessary to the thousands of decisions we make.

(Unspoken here is the reality of economic power and privilege and how it skews the concrete participation of citizens in society as market. Unmentioned, too, is that middle-strata and rich Americans, averse to thinking in terms of class, do not admit what is readily obvious; namely, that we not have and do not want a level playing field and equal opportunity whenever that might mean downward mobility for us or our children. Rhetoric that such fields exist, or are desired, may be a sop to the conscience of the affluent, and the gospel preached to those struggling to hold their ground, but it does not accord with historical and social reality. Capturing and holding markets and their benefits, not "balancing" them in some naturally harmonious competition, has always been capitalist reality.)

More needs to be said if we are to see the fit of the second bourgeois revolution with channels modernity was already cutting. The second bourgeois revolution views the world as at the disposal of self-interested individuals and groups who make and unmake relationships in accord

[38]Gary Becker, *The Economic Approach to Human Behavior* (Chicago: University of Chicago Press, 1976), 8, as cited in Wolfe, *Whose Keeper?* 39.
[39]Becker, ibid., 5, as quoted by Wolfe, ibid.

with utility. Value itself is subjective, even arbitrary, in that it rests with the subjective choices of individuals and nowhere else. In different language, all goods, including social goods, are commodities in a picture of the good life as one of "choice" and "opportunity." Freedom as "liberty" is thereby *the* reigning value, since human fulfillment happens via autonomous choices through which we fashion our own world. Citizens are entrepreneurs, producers, and consumers in the first instance, and the market is both the means of assuring a fullness of choices and the source of the logic of choice itself. This may have long been the logic of capitalism. (Thomas Jefferson already complained that republican civic virtue was losing out to the crass values of individuals pursuing their own private interests.)[40] But the second bourgeois revolution, insofar as it has succeeded, demolished the remaining barriers left in place by civil society. Indeed it doesn't take rocket-scientist intelligence to see that this logic—market logic as the dominant social logic as well—has no need for civil society, since civil society has the task of offering uncoerced associational ties through which we pursue our interests, identity, and fulfillment. Members of the Chicago School, together with millions who know neither the name nor the theory but live the practice, are clear that they have, in the market, a working substitute for civil society. All society truly requires is marketlike savvy and governmental functions that protect space for it and guarantee the procedures that allow "the magic of the market" (President Reagan's phrase) to work its wonders. This is capitalism, not as an economic form, but as a whole way of being. Society is built up from it and around it.

This said, we return to the experiment in community and society known as suburbia. Readers can judge for themselves whether an account in the *Wall Street Journal* ("Here Is the Church: As for the People, They're Picketing It") is an instance of market morality substituting for civil society. The suburb is Rancho San Diego, California, and the occasion for the feature article was the plan of Presbyterians in this "sunbaked, white-collar suburb" to build a new church.[41] The church would be the quintessential good neighbor, the exemplary community-minded suburban citizen. It would be available for community meetings from the

---

[40]See the argument and evidence in Gordon S. Wood, *The Radicalism of the American Revolution* (New York: Alfred A. Knopf, 1991).

[41]R. Gustav Niebuhr, "Here Is the Church: As for the People, They're Picketing It," *Wall Street Journal*, 20 November 1991, A1.

very outset. Day care would be offered and, if called upon, elder care. Since this growing suburb had only four churches, another place and style of worship would also serve the community's religious choices. In addition, the "dramatic, wedge-shaped building, with walls sweeping skyward and topped by a cross,"[42] would enhance the architecture of up-scale Rancho San Diego.

Yet "locals were aghast at the prospect of a church in their neighborhood."[43] Sunday traffic would interrupt peaceful weekend barbecues. Exhaust fumes spelled pollution. In streets with names like "Monaco Court" and "Teton Pass," the church's distinctive architectual style would jar a neighborhood of tidy, beige stucco houses. The upward-sweeping walls would certainly obstruct desert views. As for day care, William Rose, a thirty-three-year-old engineer, found it a nightmare: "Screaming kids in the neighborhood . . . from 7 in the morning until 6 at night."[44]

The local planning board arranged hearings, and about six months later a carefully negotiated compromise was reached. The church could be built. As a two-story boxy beige structure, it would look like the surrounding houses, thus preserving the architectural integrity of the neighborhood. There would be no dramatic steeple, just a cross placed discreetly over the door. A pledge was signed never to open a day-care center or consider elder care. James Fletcher, the developer who represented the Presbyterians, said that in the entire process, which was civil in temper and proper in its procedures, it did not matter that his client was a church. It was simply that, on balance, the community did not "*view us as an asset.*"[45]

Meanwhile the Catholic church, already built, was pressured to make concessions to conform to community tastes. It had to give up its bell tower (too loud) and limit the hours the church was open to community use (too long).[46] "There's weddings, there's funerals, there's early morning Mass, there's evening Mass, there's bingo," complained Sandy Arrington.

Rancho San Diego may or may not be typical in the particular decisions reached. The salient matter is that it is representative of local de-

[42]Ibid.
[43]Ibid.
[44]Ibid.
[45]Ibid. Emphasis mine.
[46]Ibid.

mocracy at work on a market mentality model. The decisions were made carefully and fairly, with significant community participation. They were community decisions as the summing of majority interests. The interests themselves were the outcome of a calculus of individual and collective desires, rights, and privileges. There was no debate about the common good as the community good and no serious discussion about providing for long-term moral, religious, and cultural well-being. There was only the question whether the current residents considered this prospective new resident "an asset" on the basis of privately assessed interests. It was the mentality of market logic with democracy as the frame for effective self-regarding pursuits. More than this was not needed. Nor was more desired.

Rancho San Diego is representative in another way, associated with life-style. One of the marks of modernity, many sociologists have noted, is the seemingly exponential proliferation of choice—of goods and services, of places to go and things to do, of ideas and fashions, of experiences, worldviews, even cultures and subcultures. The choices depend, of course, on one's place in the ranks of the prosperous and the aspiring prosperous. Thus when the market becomes the model of society itself and choice is closely hitched to economic means, many a suburb becomes the kind of community *Habits of the Heart* identifies as a "lifestyle enclave." Rancho San Diego is a life-style enclave, a private community with its own top-of-the-line services, from security guards to schools to supermarkets to boutiques to pools to clubs and parks.

The authors of *Habits*, with their reverence for communitarian impulses, would object to our designation of a life-style enclave as a "community" at all, though they might grudgingly accept the phrase actually used—"the *kind* of community." They reserve "community" for an inclusive whole, an interdependence of public and private life amid a variety of callings and a variety of people.[47] By contrast, "life-style" connotes essentially private life as lived around consumption choices and leisure-time activities. Life-style enclaves are thus the creations of people who share the same or similar patterns of appearance, consumption, and leisure activities.[48] Such enclaves may eventually become communities. But they do not, like

[47]Robert N. Bellah, Richard Madsen, William M. Sullivan, Ann Swidler, and Steven Tipton, *Habits of the Heart* (Berkeley and Los Angeles: University of California Press, 1985), 72.
[48]Ibid., 335.

members of true communities, initially share a history, memory, or common story. Usually their members are not very interdependent, either, in any noticeable way and do not act together except to preserve or extend the common life-style. They are look-alikes who intend to stay that way, against those who would intrude and disrupt.

Rancho San Diego is certainly more life-style enclave than community. As such it assumes formed morality and draws on whatever moral legacies its members brought with them. But it does little to provide for the moral ecology beyond the forms taken in family and school and the common life-style itself, of which family and school are themselves a large part. The rest it leaves essentially to the market mentality and the media, both powerful shapers of life-style enclaves and their moralities. Some it also leaves to the tutelage of governmental policies and the law. What it does not have or provide is any deep sense of civil society as community. It cannot, because the logic of life organized around autonomous interests provides no source or support for social solidarity. Thus community has been largely dissolved and is not even missed in any way people can identify, except as some vague lack or free-floating emptiness. Like the households of Philip Slater we will meet later, people in life-style enclaves find it very difficult to name their own unhappiness and querulousness and seem diabolically given to answering it with more of the same.

Fragmentation

LOOSE SOCIAL RELATIONS AND DISSOLVED COMMUNITY BONDS SHOULD appear in places other than suburbs if our argument is correct that modernity, especially modernity in the form of calculating market logic within democracy as interest-directed association, has undermined community, despite the valiant efforts to tuck community safely within society. The studies of boomtowns and bust towns in the 1970s serve to test the hypothesis.

The energy crisis of the 1970s brought a boomtown mentality to towns and cities in Colorado, Oklahoma, Texas, and Louisiana. The same locales later experienced decline. One would expect the period of robust activity not only to increase economic well-being but morale and "spiritual" and moral health as well. Strangely, divorce, distrust, suspicion, and general alienation tended to increase in both boomtowns and bust towns in both boom times and bust times. Economic growth certainly spawned positive consequences for the community. Yet the studies concluded that young people in particular failed to experience "rapid growth as either liberating or beneficial."[49] Crime did not increase in the boomtown phase but, curiously, fear of crime and suspiciousness did, as did antisocial behavior other than crime. Young people felt uprooted and disconnected. They felt at sea and on their own. Family life seemed to them more unstable, fragmented, disoriented. The sociologists who conducted the studies concluded that both boomtowns and bust towns undercut "the effectiveness of facilities that support informal ties such as friendliness and community spirit."[50]

One plausible argument is that because boomtowns and bust towns are both inherently disruptive, more settled seasons would yield sounder communities. Another plausible argument, however, is that the boomtown and bust town pattern is itself not an aberration in modern capitalist societies, and these economic dynamics normally strain community, often to the breaking point.

Just how fragmentary and anomic this society is then becomes an important question, since economic dynamics are the dominant ones in a society more preoccupied with economic life than any other dimension. An important religious community of a minority population is one place to test the question.

One is hard put to think of any community that has better created and preserved community bonds in the face of overwhelming odds than the black church. Racism is America's original sin, a condition regnant since the nation's inception, and the black church has always faced gravely constrained circumstances, even death threats. It was long forced to be an "invisible institution." Yet the slaves somehow managed to forge saving community in and through it. When dignity was nowhere granted in society, it was fostered in the church. When shared responsibility and participation as equals was unheard of in the world of master and slave, the church invited all to participate with whatever gifts of person were theirs. When the wider world knew no relationship that was not that of possessor and possessed, the appellations in the church were

---

[49]Wolfe, *Whose Keeper?* drawing from Richard S. Krannich, Thomas Greider, and Ronald L. Little, "Rapid Growth and Fear of Crime," *Rural Sociology* 50 (Summer 1985): 193–209.

[50]Wolfe, ibid., drawing from J. Lynn England and Stan L. Albrecht, "Boomtowns and Social Disruption," *Rural Sociology* 49 (Summer 1984): 230–46.

commonly those of brother and sister. When the economics of plantation and town were unrelentingly extractive and oppressive, the church shared goods in common, pitifully few though they often were. When outside there was only madness, strife, and pain, the church offered balm in Gilead, and with it a saving measure of solace and serenity. This was the community, sometimes the only community, where people survived with hope.[51]

This community continues. The achievements of the civil rights movement cannot be understood apart from the participation of black churches and the gifts they offered. They supplied institutional and moral support, provided indigenous leadership and funds, served as a channel of communication and a major base for recruitment. They channeled access to businesses, transportation, newspapers, colleges, and to every single generation of black families. As important as anything else, the black churches had a moral and spiritual infrastructure that refused to stop resisting injustice, combined militancy with moral forbearance and forgiveness, and schooled members in nonviolent uses of force.[52]

While by no means the only significant black institutions in the civil rights struggle, much less the only force or reason for the gains achieved, the black churches were singularly impressive as a rooted community with a rooted way of life that could, with the community's own treasures, transform itself to push aside barricades long in place. It was stirring testimony to the Spirit and to the spunk and sheer endurance of generations that this community could survive, even thrive, in a society hostile to it from the time slave boats had first landed in Atlantic harbors.

This achievement does not mean a community without serious flaws. Indeed the black church was not beyond replicating milder versions of master-slave ethics. There are good reasons that African American women have, over two centuries, now and again broken away to begin church communities of their own. Local authoritarianism, clericalism, sexism, and homophobia have been as real in black churches as white ones. Nonetheless the black churches have, against extraordinary odds, been extraordinarily successful in sustaining a cohesive community ethos over several hundred years.

---

[51]This paragraph on the black church is adapted from Larry Rasmussen, "The Public Vocation of an Eschatological Community," *Union Seminary Quarterly Review* 42, 4 (1988): 31.

[52]Lasch, *The True and Only Heaven*, 393–94.

We return to the lead-in question: How fragmentary is community now when democratic market logic prevails even in moral matters and when it substitutes for the communities of civil society?

The fine chapter "The Public Church" in *The Good Society* contains a discussion of the current reality in the black church. Some pages after Mary Hatch's insightful observation that the black church is still perhaps one of the better models for community in this society "because it stirs the imagination aesthetically, and [at the same time] moves the emotions in profoundly moral, joyous ways,"[53] there is an interview with Thomas Raskin. He notes that some black churches are as "boring and socially stifling" as white churches, but he nonetheless insists that in this society "we have to look to the church for the kinds of community that enable us to face up to our society more honestly, and impel us to find a better way to be human."[54] He goes on to observe, though, that the church has lost its identity as conservator of moral tradition and crafter of moral convictions. The entire paragraph merits careful attention:

> Reflecting on [the] black urban underclass and its growth in the past generation, Raskin warns: "We've got a generation out there on the street that is almost totally unaware of the governing symbols that shape African-American culture. We can no longer take for granted that everybody understands what exodus and exile mean for us, what crucifixion and resurrection mean. Twenty years ago a black preacher could take that for granted out in the neighborhood *and* in the pulpit. What we got now is the articulation of rage, from rap artists and from the gangs. Louis Farrakhan speaks that language, too, when he says, We have no investment here. We are a separate people. We have to do for ourselves. Even he pulls a version of Dale Carnegie striving for success: 'Pull yourself up by your own bootstraps.' But he can say nothing about what it means to share space, and make a world where black and white can live together in justice. This is a kind of rage that doesn't trust anybody, that doesn't reach out any further than the other members of the gang. The crips and the bloods—that's my only family, that's my only community."[55]

[53]Bellah et al., *The Good Society*, 208.
[54]Ibid., 212.
[55]Ibid., 213.

Even apart from Raskin's lament about the loss of the church as a community of moral content around key Christian symbols and narrative, and apart from his description of the rage of the growing underclass, the striking parallel, seemingly bizarre at first, is that of Louis Farrakhan and Dale Carnegie. Wildly different personalities speaking from and to vastly different circumstances, they are both quintessentially U.S. American in a key aspect of their moral creed: "We have to do for ourselves." Neither knows about moral community in society, that is, "about what it means to share space, and make a world where black and white can live together in justice." If this paragraph is reread, this time dropping the black underclass and its rage, and substituting white youth living for the moment in Carnegie's neighborhood, curiously parallel results emerge: "we have to do for ourselves" and the whitened version of "the crips and the bloods—that's my only family, that's my only community."

Of course it matters immensely whether one is black or white in this society. Farrakhan says of African Americans, We are a separate people who must pull ourselves up by our own bootstraps and can trust nobody because this society has been racist from the beginning and unrelentingly hostile to black well-being for four centuries. By contrast, white disciples of Carnegie find this society user-friendly. All the more striking, then, is the parallel moral creed—"we're on our own"—and the slow unraveling of traditional moral communities. In Dr. King's dream turned ironic, black and white together are now living from moral fragments only, as we are living from community fragments, and neither has sufficient bulk in the moral life to effect even a fair society, say nothing of a good one.

Eric Lincoln and Lawrence Mamiya's monumental study *The Black Church in the African American Experience*, throws light on this. After noting that black churches continue to be the central institutional sector in most black communities, have higher rates of church attendance than white Protestants, and suffer less decline in membership,[56] the authors address "the challenge of two black Americas and two black churches."[57] It seems that both those African Americans who have benefited economically through education and career achievements made possible by the civil rights struggle and those who have become part of the growing urban underclass are less churched than other African Americans. Mid-

[56]C. Eric Lincoln and Lawrence H. Mamiya, *The Black Church in the American Experience* (Durham and London: Duke University Press, 1990), 382.
[57]Ibid., 383.

dle-strata black young adults live out the patterns of college graduates in general, and the underclass knows all about the rage Raskin speaks of, yet without finding the church as their core community. The challenge to the black church, the authors write, is to reach across the expanding class boundaries and growing fragmentation among African Americans and to solidify demographic changes in black communities as those communities scatter more widely across ravaged urban areas.

The difficulty of doing this, especially reaching out to the urban poor, is highlighted in the discussion of black families. "The black family is the primary unit of the Black Church"[58] because of "a symbiosis between the black family and the church which makes for mutual reinforcement and creates for most black families their initial or primary identity."[59] Yet the tests involving black children in the 1980s on self-esteem and cultural identity show levels that have slid back to those observed by Kenneth and Mamie Clark prior to the Supreme Court desegregation decision of 1954. Family crises of another sort are reflected in very high rates of incarceration among young black males and high rates of teenage pregnancy among females.[60] What is happening here, to read between the lines, is not simply the toll of poverty, real as that is. It is cultural destruction and social nihilism in the streets.

When the realities of black family life in the city are put side by side with the fragmentation of the black community along class lines, the churches are up against obstacles as formidable as any in history. Lincoln and Mamiya draw the tally near the end of their study.

> Today's Black Church is struggling for relevance in the resolution of today's black problems: racism; drug abuse; child care; health and welfare; housing; counseling; unemployment; teenage pregnancy; the false securities of conspicuous consumption; and the whole tragic malaise with which society in general is burdened. [The Black Church] must address all these social challenges without abandoning its distinctive mandate to assist human beings in their efforts to find conciliation and comfort

[58]Ibid., 402.
[59]Ibid.
[60]Ibid., 402–3.

> with their Creator. There is no moratorium on the human need for spiritual and moral nurture.[61]

Differently said, the black churches' experience of society is one in which they must both address an array of social problems and simultaneously create and sustain nurturing community. In an increasingly fragmented community and world, they must undertake everything at once. They remain formidable communities themselves, but they live from community fragments and moral fragments in daily danger of further loss. If this is so for institutions as historically cohesive as these, and the alternatives (for the well-off) are life-style enclaves in the manner of Rancho San Diego, then the prognosis for this society's health is grim.

Double Loss

SUCH HAS BEEN THE HARD JOURNEY OF COMMUNITY IN ITS CONTINUOUS tussle with modernity. The final outcome is uncertain, since community has both changed and survived. Some genuinely communal fragments remain, and innumerable clusters of associational ties still bind us together. But community's health as the moral locus for learning virtues for public life is frail and failing. Already insecure, the triumph of the second bourgeois revolution dealt community health a disabling blow, at least in the United States. Since community is the concrete shape of grace for most people most of the time, and all people at important times, this is crippling damage. The most serious damage is not what many claim, however—the moral rehabilitation in the 1980s of certain repugnant vices: greed, desire, ambition. The order and hold of the vices and virtues rises and falls across society's changing moral seasons, and the day may soon come when, in the manner typical of a faddish society, these are out rather than in. But swings of the moral pendulum will not change the nature of the true damage. The true damage is retaining those dynamics that erode and threaten to destroy the communities that do moral formation in the first place. The matrix and process of basic moral formation—real people with real histories in real communities with definite moral tasks—is what has been put on society's endangered species list, not simply this or that value or virtue.

[61]Ibid., 398.

In short, we flirt with the disaster of society-without-community. More precisely, the erosion of civil society means a "post-public society"[62] in which few base communities exist to do moral formation for life together as interdependent strangers—modernity's very trademark. Thus far in the battle with modernity, then, community has lost. It is tattered and beaten, though far from ready to check itself into the morgue. But modernity has lost as well. It has lost the wellsprings of the moral character it depends on for its own existence. It has lost its own incubator, laboratory, and training ground. It needs what only certain kinds of communities can provide, but it destroys them. And the truth be known, society-without-community is as confining and uninhabitable as community-without-society is constraining and oppressive. In light of the second bourgeois revolution especially, Wolfe's question, "Can bourgeois society [now] survive bourgeois man?"[63] is the right one.[64]

---

[62]The phrase is Christian T. Iosso's from his chapter "Changes in Ecumenical Public Witness, 1967–1990," in *The Church's Public Role*, ed. Dieter Hessel (Grand Rapids, Mich.: Wm. B. Eerdmans, 1992).

[63]Wolfe, *Whose Keeper?* 27.

[64]Dennis P. McCann's review of Robert B. Reich's *Work of Nations: Preparing Ourselves for Twenty-first-Century Capitalism* (New York: Alfred A. Knopf, 1991) includes the following citation from Reich: "The question is whether the habits of citizenship are sufficiently strong to withstand the centrifugal forces of the new global economy. Is there enough of simple loyalty to place—of civic obligation, even when unadorned by enlightened self-interest—to elicit sacrifice nonetheless? We are, after all, citizens as well as economic actors; we may work in markets but we live in societies. How tight is the social and political bond when the economic bond unravels?" Quoted in Dennis P. McCann, "Justice and Economics in the Twenty-first Century," *Christian Century* 108, 31 (1991): 1007.

CHAPTER 4

Market and State as Moral Proxies

Society as Market, Society as State

MANY WOULD NOT SHARE THE TONE OF THE FOREGOING PAGES. APOCALYPSE and near hysteria are misplaced. So is, they say, the "profound concern" that surfaces in every blue-ribbon commission report on the family, education, youth, the city, or the nation's farm communities. Against the gloom and doom that periodically ups the volume of American blue funk, calm reason knows there are ways to arrange effective moral agency without relying on the changing and uncertain remnants of civil society. Society on the model of the market can muster most of what is required, and society on the model of the state can do the rest, supplemented with expanding international agreements and institutions. This is, in fact, what the experiment of modernity is finally about. Democratic capitalism, to name the example that has triumphed, has the polity and the economy to accomplish all that is required, from a moral point of view. Liberty and equality, if well balanced and regulated, suffice as well as anything for the good society, and market and state together are their means.

Such has been the promise, the working creed, and the practice of recent modernity, whether openly stated or not. (Sometimes it is openly stated. Francis Fukuyama's *The End of History and the Last Man* even argues the irreversibility of liberal democratic capitalist societies as the solution to world ills.)[1]

---

[1]See the argument of Francis Fukuyama, *The End of History and the Last Man*

There are good reasons why modernity has unloaded so much into the ample laps of market and state. The chief one has already been noted: If we share a common space and a common destiny on a fragile and imperiled planet, we cannot rely on local communities and networks of voluntary organizations as the only effective moral agents. Their reach, however impressive, is insufficient in a world of millions of interdependent strangers whom we will never know or even see, but who shape our lives as we do theirs. Positioning the moral life in face-to-face relationships surely cannot serve society at large, then, however personally fulfilling it may be for many people. Other agents will have to do what society must; namely, regulate behavior and address our obligations to one another as gathered foreigners who occupy a public space together and share limited resources under constrained conditions. Only the transpersonal agencies of the "systems-world," of the economy and the state, have the wherewithal to coordinate that which is necessary to meet needs across wide, complex expanses. We must have frameworks and mechanisms—the state, the market—that the associational ties of civil society do not provide.

The modern market, for example, is an institution able to outstrip any network of communities in creating a spontaneous and dynamic order from millions of independent, decentralized decisions.[2] Neither a network of communities nor the state can by conscious decision begin to match the market's ability to allocate resources. It utterly charms its worshipers and critics alike by achieving a degree of order and efficiency independent of human goodness, government coercion, or even extensive knowledge.

(New York: Free Press, 1992). This is a provocative but very bad book. Despite its endorsement by people who should know better—George Will, Charles Krauthammer, Irving Kristol—history will soon render it quaint. Not only does it misinterpret its main source, Hegel, apparently ignoring his writing on the very subject of the book's concern, namely, the state, but it ignores the chief challenge to democratic capitalism as an enduring arrangement—fragile ecosystems and limits that industrial society and high levels of consumption have flouted with abandon. Anyone who writes of the "irreversibility" of our polity and economy but who ignores the ecocrisis is standing in a strange place, somewhere outside our present history itself.

[2]Herman E. Daly and John B. Cobb, Jr., *For the Common Good: Redirecting the Economy toward Community, the Environment, and a Sustainable Future* (Boston: Beacon Press, 1989), 44.

This necessary coordination is not the only reason the market draws. Society with the vigor of capitalist markets released millions from the grip of various command economies and societies, from fuedalism and aristocracy to communism, and in the process extended freedom and fostered creativity. This is as much a moral achievement as an economic and political one. Granted, capitalist markets are anticommunal. But the communities they often break up—to recall Marx—are frequently restrictive, suffocating ones devoid of opportunity for new worlds. Modern market society has also meant an enormous advance in generating wealth, not just freedom. Since what is not produced cannot be distributed, this, too, is an achievement of moral scope and substance. In a world that is technically capable of producing enough, hunger and unmet material need are moral crimes. The market is the engine that can produce the wealth to address such crimes.

Yet there has been persistent and deep injustice in market societies. To be more precise, we should say capitalist market societies. Since all modern economies use markets, it is important to remember that it was to address the failures of the inordinate power of capitalism's market dynamics—unemployment, poverty, homelessness, extremes of wealth and income, disruption of close communities, and so on—that the state was deemed a moral counterforce. Capitalism, to be sure, opposed slavery as an element of a fuedal and aristocratic caste system and welcomed the free movement of labor. But it also exploited that labor and produced wage slaves instead. Furthermore it showed little care for any who were unable to enter a dynamic job market or were too disadvantaged to push into the ranks of the entrepreneurs. Indeed everything that fell outside capitalist markets was labeled an externality and left out of the economy's consideration, whether that was people or ecosystems.

Persistent injustice in capitalist market societies, then, is what led many to organize and call upon the state. The state answered the call and either commanded the high moral ground on its own, with a command economy, or complemented a system of markets with regulations in order to do what markets, left alone, fail to do well: regulate public goods (roads, national defense, education, parks, etc.); address "externalities" (the consequences of market activity that do not lend themselves to a market solution—greenhouse gases and acid rain, for example, or black lung disease); affect distribution in the direction of a more just society (the market's efficient allocation of resources does not guarantee, or even imply, their just distribution); maintain the conditions of competition itself (economic power tends to be concentrated as a result of markets so that winners grow and losers disappear; thus it is necessary to reestablish the very conditions of competition on which efficient markets depend);[3] and counter the social injustices of racism, sexism, homophobia, and so on, which markets neglect or exacerbate.

Thus while there are considerable differences among the welfare capitalist societies of Europe, the established socialist societies on several continents, and the social policy society of this nation, all of them share the conviction that the state is a moral proxy or a moral agent for meeting obligations en masse through the instrumentalities of law and bureaucracy.

Not that the state would have been absent if markets had been more efficient. As mentioned, the nation-state has been a fixture of modernity since the Peace of Westphalia in 1648. It has had its strongest and most influential voices in Rousseau and Hegel and their disciples on both the right and left, a parallel to Smith and his case that markets are good for society. Indeed Hegel and Rousseau understood the nation-state as the community of the modern epoch and as the adequate substitute for premodern communities. The state, in their widely appropriated view, is a rational legal entity subjecting everyone to the rule of law and emphasizing the subordination of the individual to this ultimate form of political association. Hegel especially gave the corporate state unqualified freedom and was even scornful of individual rights as a domain the state should not invade. In his scheme, markets would be allowed sufficient play to modernize society, but the state would finally control economic life. Only the state, after all, can unite the particular and the universal and serve the people as a whole in their own name. It is thus in the province of the state alone that the Idea of Freedom (Hegel), and so of the ethical life, can be realized. The state, then, is the supreme moral community. It is the place where the varied interests of civil society itself are finally realized and its conflicts resolved.[4]

Rousseau's argument was a moral one as well. Citizenship for him was essentially moral agency. Through the state as the source of common identity and social inclusion, citizens could develop their capacity as agents of their own collective life together. While not Hegel's state, Rousseau's shared modernity's conviction that identity as citizens of a state and nation could substitute for the identities forged in less inclusive

[3]Ibid., 49–60.
[4]Hegel's argument is elaborated at greatest length in *Philosophy of Right*.

communities.[5] "Republicanism" and its civic virtue, if widely practiced, would render society coherent and cohesive on a universal basis.

A variety of imperatives, a lot of history, and some articulate spokespersons, then, have made the turn to market and state compelling for matters of the moral life. The specific question here is not, however, one of general moral legitimacy. Much less is it a futile exercise in imagination—how might modernity have looked otherwise? The question is about the concrete outcome of this history. What has society as nation-state and market meant for moral communities? What emerge as the broadbrush consequences for the moral life?

Common Outcomes

ONE OF THE CHIEF CONSEQUENCES, ALREADY MENTIONED IN PASSING, must be elaborated. When the market became the model of society itself and not a segment of society only, that is, when capitalism became a culture and a society and not simply the means for economic exchange—society drew on a morality it failed to reproduce and undermined the communities that provided that morality in the first place. As already noted, capitalism has from the first taken the communities of civil society for granted, in order to generate its necessary moral capital, much as it has taken for granted that the biosphere would regenerate the natural capital. Yet it undermined both and has not effectively restored the depleted capital of either nature or moral community.

Ironically this neglect of its moral accounts and the health of their source communities has meant the development, quite against the official ideology, of an elaborately bureaucratized and expensive society. Why? Because society could not handle in more informal ways the array of problems any society faces when its human bonds are atomized and its moral base thinned to a mere veneer of what is needed. The supposedly freest society then becomes the most litigious one; and a region known for its no-holds-barred, deregulated individualism, the Los Angeles basin of southern California, turns out to be a region strapped with innumerable regulations. Fully against all its own intentions, professionalized interest-group bureaucracy has become the political form of the second bourgeois revolution and its morality-eroding market mentality. Capital-

[5]See the discussion by Michael Walzer in "The Idea of Civil Society," *Dissent* Spring 1991, 294–95.

ist society in this form becomes bureaucratized because the market fails to provide society a moral guidance system of its own.

The sheer cost of this is staggering. If it is mildly true that crime doesn't pay, it is true with a vengeance that a society suffering the breakdowns that stem from moral collapse faces a long list of expensive social problems. Adequate protection and security, or the price of enacting and enforcing laws and regulations aimed to check abuse and corruption in business and government, or the social welfare check for domestic violence and unwanted children or spouses, or the cleanup costs for willfully violating the environment, or the loss of public revenues through cheating on taxes—these only begin to tally the cost of neglecting moral community.

To this must be added that the state as model for society strangely suffered much the same outcome. This has starkly been the case for societies now suffering the drift and pain of the collapse of society-as-socialist-state. The socialist nations had tried to provide comprehensive moral formation. They dictated the substance of education, including moral education. They supplied rites and rituals for human passage: for birth, puberty, marriage, retirement, and death, together with a string of socialist "holy" days, heroes, and special observances. They designated the forms and recipients of charity and tried on all fronts to face the full range of human needs. They reached farther into family life and the monitoring of voluntary organizations than any previous governments. They told farmers how to farm, teachers how to teach, doctors how to doctor, and writers how to write. It was perhaps the most comprehensive effort ever made to institutionalize moral obligation under governmental auspices and control. For reasons we will long be studying, it failed on a scale commensurate with its own bulk and reach and in keeping with "a soteriological myth" no less pretentious.[6] Most ironic of all, this kind of socialism did few things as badly as socialization itself.

In the course of studying the moral failure of central command socialism, the conservatives' critique will be heard again and again with new force. That argument, it should be recalled, was a moral one. It was not simply the contention that socialism was economically inefficient. The conservatives' bible, Friedrich Hayek's *Road to Serfdom*, says it well and, it should be added, means to extend its point beyond establishment

[6]The phrase, "a soteriological myth" is Lesek Kolakowski's as cited by Seligman, *The Idea of Civil Society* (New York: The Free Press, 1992) 57.

socialism. Hayek holds in disdain any state with "extensive government control," any "nanny state" that peers into the nooks and crannies of citizens' lives and leads them by the hand.[7]

> The most important change which extensive government control produces is a psychological change, an alteration in the character of the people. . . . The will of [people] is not shattered but softened, bent and guided; [people] are seldom forced by it to act, but they are constantly restrained from acting. Such a power does not destroy, but it prevents existence; it does not tyrannize, but it compresses, enervates, extinguishes, and stupifies a people, till each nation is reduced to be nothing better than a flock of timid and industrial animals, of which government is the shepherd.[8]

What Hayek and conservatives overlook, however, is that the market, too, dulls the sense of moral responsibility and agency and "produces . . . a psychological change, an alteration in the character of the people." It does so in a quite different way, in the name of the reified market which seems to belong to the natural order itself and to a human nature naturally given to life lived in keeping with calculating self-interest. This deflects the realization that markets and "the market" are human social constructs meticulously arranged to facilitate exchange, which, for that reason, are subject to moral assessment and choice at every level. In everyday discourse this is obscured, the social relations of production are mystified, and the actual choices "markets make" (!) are not perceived as human moral choices. In turn this leads to the defense, on grounds of economic "necessity" and the unchanging elements of "human nature," of all manner of repugnant social and moral outcomes. Such defense numbs, even denies, people's sense of their own moral agency, responsibility, and accountability. That conservatives join central command socialists in this outcome is another fine irony. To make the market the whole of the city, rather than one of its zones, and to subject all of life to the morality of the bazaar had much the same impact

---

[7]The phrase "nanny state" is itself not Hayek's but that of his avid and immensely influential admirer Milton Friedman. See Friedman's use of it, among other places, in his biting criticism of President Bush for not consistently pursuing Reagan's government-hands-off economic policy: Milton Friedman, "Oodoov Economics," *New York Times*, 2 February 1992, E17.

[8]Cited in Gar Alperowitz, "Building a Saving Democracy," *Sojourners* 19 (July 1990): 12.

on people's sense of moral agency as the statist extreme conservatives passionately sought to counter.[9]

As if to pile ironies one upon another, market society, with its impersonal efficiency and reliance on imperious egoism, and state society, with its impersonal social policy and reliance on imperious state responsibility, both failed to reproduce the moral base they needed in the citizenry, just as they both failed to deliver what they both promised to achieve in their very different ways—the common good! Neither of its own accord mustered the very morality it depended on—civility, loyalty, social solidarity, trust in authority, competence, and consideration in human relations. Indeed the unarticulated despair in so many quarters now is that just when social problems must somehow be addressed en masse, the socialization process requisite for civil existence itself is in shambles everywhere—in capitalist, socialist, and former socialist societies alike. While from the point of view of competing cold war ideologies, democratic capitalism won and command socialism lost, from the point of view of a moral assessment, the socialist experiment is but a worse-case scenario of moral deficiencies that capitalist societies face in high degree. Both sides in the cold war depleted the soils of nature and community.

So it may be that just when Western democracy and capitalism celebrate their triumph over the communist alternative, they find their own systems gradually unraveling in the way Octavio Paz predicted.[10] This is why there is an eery familiarity in the remarks of the former president of a small central European nation with its own proud traditions of (earlier) democracy and its own (forced) experiment with command socialism. We quote Václav Havel at length:

> The return of freedom to a place that became morally unhinged has produced something that it clearly had to produce, and therefore something we might have expected. But it has turned out to be far more serious than anyone could have predicted: an enormous and blindingly visible explosion of every imaginable human vice. A wide range of questionable or at least ambivalent human tendencies, quietly encouraged over the years and, at the same time, quietly pressed to serve the daily operation of the to-

[9]Michael Walzer, *Spheres of Justice* (New York: Basic Books, 1983), 108–16.
[10]See the first few pages of chap. 1.

> talitarian system, has suddenly been liberated, as it were, from its straitjacket and given free rein at last. The authoritarian regime imposed a certain order—if that is the right expression for it—on these vices (and in doing so "legitimized" them, in a sense). This order has now been broken down, but a new order that would limit rather than exploit these vices, an order based on a freely accepted responsibility to and for the whole of society, has not yet been built; nor could it have been, for such an order takes years to develop and cultivate.
>
> And thus we are witnesses to a bizarre state of affairs: society has freed itself, true, but in some ways it behaves worse than when it was in chains. Criminality has grown rapidly, and the familiar sewage that in times of historical reversal always wells up from the nether regions of the collective psyche has overflowed into the mass media, especially the gutter press. But there are other, more serious and dangerous, symptoms: hatred among nationalities, suspicion, racism, even signs of fascism; vicious demagogy, intrigue, and deliberate lying; politicking, an unrestrained, unheeding struggle for purely particular interests, a hunger for power, unadulterated ambition, fanaticism of every imaginable kind; new and unprecedented varieties of robbery, the rise of different mafias; the general lack of tolerance, understanding, taste, moderation, reason.[11]

Havel goes on to discuss "genuine politics" and to commit himself to its realization in Czechoslovakia (now two states). The moral grounds are crucial.

> Genuine politics, politics worthy of the name, and in any case the only politics that I am willing to devote myself to, is simply serving those close to oneself: serving the community, and serving those who come after us. Its deepest roots are moral because it is a responsibility, expressed through action, to and for the whole, a responsibility that is what it is—a "higher" responsibility, which grows out of a conscious or subconscious certainty that our death ends nothing, because everything is forever being recorded and evaluated somewhere else, somewhere "above us,"

[11]Václav Havel, "Paradise Lost," *New York Review of Books* 39, 7 (1992): 6.

> in what I have called "the memory of Being," an integral aspect of the secret order of the cosmos, of nature, and of life, which believers call God and to whose judgment everything is liable.[12]

In sum, we are clearly confronted with the need to develop another way of thinking about moral formation and obligation than those represented by this century's chief models of society—society-as-market and society-as-state. These recent massive modern experiments have not garnered sufficient moral substance by way of either the market's rational quest of self-interest or the state's coercive external authority. Both have lamed the moral sources of civil society. The question is not whether there will be markets and states for the foreseeable future and whether they will be morally significant actors. They will. But they cannot do what only more intimate, personal congeries of relationships can. What they can do, and have done in a negative vein, is dumb down a personal sense of moral agency and responsibility. They have allowed relatively little scope for people to develop their own moral capacities in the steady company of others and have substituted either the rules of market transaction or the rules of policy and law for the struggles of moral freedom and accountability. Under these circumstances, rules and procedures and the bounds of legality come to mean more for the moral life of citizens than learning moral maturity through the exercise of personal moral agency in the presence of strangers. Rules in fact now act as substitutes for the moral socialization only civil society can adequately provide. In short, the question is how modernity's strangers can muster the social practices and settings by which they come to know and live by the morality they themselves have created.

Community's Contribution

THE ABSENCE OF THESE PRACTICES AND SETTINGS LEAVES US DUMBfounded when we come upon new and difficult moral issues (a dilemma in biomedical ethics, for example) or when an old moral issue assumes high public profile and demands national attention (abortion, for example, or any number of other issues around women's reproductive rights). Given the disabling of so many moral communities, the public is left

[12]Ibid.

only the options of market and state rules and the thin stratum of moral possibilities they offer.

Perhaps this is why an issue with a history in the modern era, say, a matter of political economy, finds supporters of the state predictably on the left and those who favor the market on the right. But a new moral issue (a biomedical one) or a newly public one (abortion) might well find the free market favored by the left and strict government regulation favored by the right. No doubt there are many and complex reasons for switching in order to fight. But one may be that, having lost much of civil society's contribution to public life, the moral imagination of people is reduced to only two ways of considering social and moral obligations. When one of them (pick market or state) doesn't work, the only recourse is to flip to the other. In a richer moral environment, the laboratory of civil society could serve to move us all beyond polarized choices—"pro-choice," "pro-life"; or "leave it to the market," "leave it to the government." But civil moral community is neither cared for nor called on.

What precisely can the communities of civil society—that is, communities of affection, friendship, voluntary action, family, faith, and education—accomplish that state and market as moral proxies cannot? In its detail that is the subject of a later chapter, but it can be anticipated here.

Boundaries between "community" and "society" are admittedly porous in the modern world because of the widespread existence and use of associational ties (ties among casual acquaintances around matters of common interest and welfare). As we shall later argue, this easy movement between communitarian and associational ties holds promise. Nonetheless, it is largely by way of relatively intact, small-scale communities with some staying power that we learn trust, temper individualism as a moral style, agree to freely serve, hone leadership skills for work together, have and raise children, learn to give to charities, volunteer for dirty, difficult, and unpleasant jobs, clean up after ourselves, restrain appetites, take out the garbage, help friends, care for siblings, parents, children, relatives, and friends, learn to read, learn to return books to the library, observe meaning-giving traditions, receive all manner of moral direction, including basic moral rules and social etiquette, find out by increments what moral responsibility means from childhood up, develop qualities of character, practice decision making, acquire a moral language, nurture moral sensibilities, take responsibility for a pet, plant, or sibling, recover from serious mistakes, find our first models of behavior, and, most important, learn to forgive and start anew. In a word, we discover in microcosm how the bewildering world works and how to find our way in it.[13]

Such only begins the list! Some items may never be learned, of course—a serious failure that redounds negatively to the larger society. But this suffices to show that while civil society has been trespassed on by both market and state, it still has functions in the moral life that market and state cannot of themselves supply sufficiently well even when they are indispensable to the moral life itself. By way of unintentional understatement, Alan Wolfe says the practices of civil society are "a kind of trial heat" for the more difficult business "of taking the perspective of future generations, responding to the needs of strangers, or learning to live within diverse cultures."[14] They are certainly a trial heat. But they are more. They are the decades-long training program as well.

Briefly, then, modernity's grand moral experiments—market and state as the dominant models for society itself—have extended moral obligation to millions of people in ways local communities could not and cannot. They have also rescued significant populations from the whims and crude injustices of entrenched local ways of life, in the process transforming traditional behavioral patterns and setting them on a new level of dignity and respect. Advances in human rights and the extension of the franchise in many places in the world are instances of great moral victories; neither had any sizable audience in premodern communities. Of late, millennia of patriarchy and homophobia have been significantly chipped away; again, this is the work of modern currents running counter to the life realities of traditional communities. The gains of the civil rights movement as written into law was mentioned earlier; but the indispensable role of the state battling entrenched racist elements of traditional local communities was not.

So no one wants to deny that modernity has achieved its own worthy moral capital—individual freedom, human rights, critical thought itself, tolerance, voluntary association—which has now become part of the moral endowment we draw on. But society-as-market and society-as-state have thinned moral obligation in the process of extending it and exhausted large deposits of the moralities they inherited.

---

[13]Alan Wolfe, *Whose Keeper? Social Science and Moral Obligation* (Berkeley, Los Angeles, and London: University of California Press, 1989), 189. I have drawn from Wolfe but freely added to his list.

[14]Ibid., 233.

Worse, they undermined the communities that supplied those moralities. For all these reasons, market and state now serve up the urgent requirement to think anew about how to do moral formation in the modern-postmodern world at the same time that they present a numbing array of social and moral problems to be addressed without delay.

Enlightenment Ethics

NOTES ABOUT THE DISCIPLINE OF CHRISTIAN ETHICS SHOULD BE POSTED here. They may pale in significance compared with what we have just described but they are important for the later discussion of the church's resources as a community of moral formation and conviction.

The first is the observation that the major traditions of moral philosophy developed since the Enlightenment, and thus the major ethical theories of modernity, move as intellectual traditions along the lines just sketched for morality in society. Utilitarianism (associated with John Stuart Mill and Jeremy Bentham) and Kantianism both depend on a substantial moral inheritance they do not provide for nor much acknowledge. Although very different from each other and commonly viewed as the contrasting options of modern Western ethics, both utilitarianism and Kantianism operate on the basis of moral rules, principles and procedures whose appeal rests in a moral deposit they evidently take for granted. It is as though Mill, Bentham, Kant, and their respective disciples all anticipated a later contention they prematurely subscribed to as sufficient moral theory: the contention that "good games depend on good rules more than they depend on good players."[15] Kant himself argued straightforwardly that good constitutions made for a good citizenry.[16] At the same time, these venerable traditions must surely have known that the players, and no one else, make the rules and keep, change, or disregard them. Yet these formative thinkers seem not to have taken account of this in their theories. They assumed the ethics of character but did not pro-

---

[15]Ibid., 122, citing H. Geoffrey Brennan and James M. Buchanan, *The Reason of Rules: Constitutional Political Economy* (Cambridge: Cambridge University Press, 1985), 150.

[16]See the discussion in Larry Rasmussen, "Law and Morality, Morality and Law," *Dialog* 9 (1970): 249–56. Neglect of the ethics of formation is helpfully discussed by Susan Moller Okin in *Justice, Gender, and the Family* (New York: Basic Books, 1991), 17ff.

vide for it in truly substantial ways. Here they replicated modernity's naive expropriation of civil society and its communities of moral formation. Communities of civil society make the players who make and keep, change and break, the rules. Perhaps Kant, Bentham, and company simply forgot that we are children before we are adults and that the moral life does not begin in "reason" but in childhood!

Prominent options in moral theory echo modernity in another closely related way. The Enlightenment sought the universally human, some fundamental core that could be stripped of particularity and exist independently of differences generated by race, gender, class, and culture. Moral appeal could be made to the shared faculty of "reason" in a way that permitted universal moral norms and procedures. But more than this, the provincialities of traditional communities and cultures were held in veiled contempt as tribal residues in a world verging on true cosmopolitanism. Family, religious, ethnic, and regional loyalties were something we were to outgrow, or at least subordinate to more encompassing considerations. Particularistic commitments were suspect, as were local and traditional ties.[17] The Enlightenment's world was also a secularizing one, so moral principles and procedures would require no foundation in the contentious ways of religion. We could and would be good without God. The prominent ethical theories thus not only assumed civil society's supply of moral persons, they also assumed a cosmopolitanism and secularization they regarded as moral enlightenment. This intensified modernity's disdain for what Harvey Cox, in his unrestrained celebration of modernity's ethic as a Christian ethic, *The Secular City*, calls the outmoded social forms of "tribe and town."[18] Because of this bias for the universal, cosmopolitan, and secular in modern ethical

---

[17]This discussion is from George Scialabba's fine review of Christopher Lasch's *True and Only Heaven*. See "From Enlightenment to Redemption" in *Christianity and Crisis* 51, 16/17 (1991): 351–54.

[18]Harvey Cox, *The Secular City: A Celebration of Its Liberties and an Invitation to Its Discipline* (New York: Macmillan, 1965), 6. Citing Cox here does not mean he retained this unqualified endorsement of modernity. He did not, as later works make clear. That, of course, does not alter either the perspective recorded in *The Secular City* or the influence this volume exercised for a decade and more. A similar comment can be made about the note below on John Rawls's *Theory of Justice*. Rawls has since written insightfully about community in our lives. But that does not change the anthropology and social theory, or the initial strong influence, of *A Theory of Justice*.

theory, even Christian ethics has paid little attention to particular ways of life as the substance of ethics. At the level of working theory, it, too, has shied from concrete community as the subject, as if the only thing to be found there would be unsavory tribal residues.

Finally, these modern ethical theories, different as they are, rest in a common notion of the human self that cannot be sustained given our social nature. They assume a unified self that exists prior to the actions it contemplates and, for that matter, prior to the context of those actions. It is doubtful that any of us possesses a unified self at any time. We are always trying to get it together. Together or not, we certainly do not exist separate from and prior to the places where we are in the continual process of becoming. Nor are we ever separate from and prior to whatever actions we contemplate and take. The notion of an independent, transcendent ego is fallacious. Nonetheless even much-applauded recent works in ethics, such as John Rawls's *Theory of Justice*, perpetuate this modern error of treating a self separate from its constitutive, highly particular communities.[19]

Another note on modernity and ethics is necessary and related. The turn in Christian ethics of late to "character formation" and "community" as primary concerns is no idiosyncratic preoccupation of a few quirky, underemployed professional ethicists. It is the rather late response to the growing sense that the moral formation of society at the base is in crisis most everywhere—north, south, east, west, from sea to shining sea; and to the sense that the going models of society, society as market and state, are failing us. Of lesser but real importance, it is also a sharp reaction to the deficits of the broad Enlightenment legacy in ethics.

---

[19]See Iris Young's discussion in "The Ideal of Community and the Politics of Difference," in *Feminism/Postmodernism*, ed. Linda J. Nicholson (New York and London: Routledge, 1990), 322, n. 18. Young is reporting Michael Sandel's critique of John Rawls in Sandel's *Liberalism and the Limits of Justice* (Cambridge: Cambridge University Press, 1982). I have appropriated that discussion for this criticism of the lingering Enlightenment anthropology in modern ethical options. Young herself argues against community and unwittingly remakes the same argument for "the unoppressive city" as the ideal that Harvey Cox presented in greater detail in *The Secular City*. I think Young is exactly right in her criticisms of community as a *model* for society and her dismissal of traditional communities organized around unity anchored in homogeneity. She is wrong, however, to dismiss it altogether. She leaves unanswered the crucial issue of how moral formation happens even for the citizens who inhabit her "unoppressive city."

In a word, while Christian ethics owes a great debt to the morally progressive traditions of modernity, and desperately needed to be extricated from romantic and reactionary attachment to traditional communities and their moral patterns, at crucial points it acculturated to modernity at too high a price. The crucial points are in fact the same ones that litter the history sketched here from the beginnings of modernity to the present. What conservative, liberal, and socialist variants of modernity all have in common, from Adam Smith to Ronald Reagan and the fall of state socialism, and from Kant and Hegel through Rawls, is the principled neglect and sometimes outright destruction of the very community sources of morality they and all society depend on.

CHAPTER 5

Present Currents

The Device Paradigm

THE WORKINGS OF MODERNITY UPON MORALITY AND COMMUNITY cannot be fathomed apart from the impact of science and technology. To consider the reigning models of society alone and the erosion of community by a dynamic and changing capitalism is not enough. More is involved.

Science, with its powerful ability to explain, hypothesize, and test, and technology, with its transformative capacities, are as much the furnishings of modernity as capitalism, socialism, democracy, and the nation-state. Indeed the liberation dream of modernity probably owes more to science and technology's promise to bring the forces of nature under control than to any other single element. All moderns, whether capitalists or socialists, democrats or totalitarians, have stood by scientific technology and its horizon of promise.

Nonetheless a long-standing and sometimes acrimonious debate continues about the impact of scientific technology on society. Is it a salvatory power, a demonic one, or sheer neutral instrumentality? Is it *the* shaper of our world, including our values and manner of thinking, or only an impressive ensemble of tools we direct in accord with values and visions independent of it?

In any event, the debate has been better at making general claims about the influence of scientific technology than it has in explaining the actual social dynamic and its particular grammar. Since explaining in detail and with precision how things work is science's vocation par excellence, this omission is another irony.

One exception to this lacuna in the debate is Albert Borgmann and his description of "the device paradigm" as the grammar of technology's social workings. As Adam Smith was a moral philosopher who described the economic dynamics of what later became capitalism, Borgmann is a moral philosopher who exposits technology's social influence. His exegesis in *Technology and the Character of Contemporary Life* follows.

Borgmann's analysis is subtle, complex, and requires patience. It may be well, then, to begin with the conclusion and use it as a guide. With an exposition of "the device paradigm," Borgmann argues that our relationship to modern technology not only defines most economic relations but profoundly shapes our social and moral relations in general. We treat an expanding range of human relationships, as well as things, as commodities whose utility we measure and consume. The conclusion is that society on the device paradigm provides remarkably little scope for people to develop their own moral capacities and paradoxically leaves them feeling powerless just when many of their choices and powers have multiplied greatly. This condition stems from scientific technology's applauded achievements as modernity's wondrous tool kit.

Furthermore, and even more important, society living the device paradigm dissolves many of the moral networks that grow up around the familiar reference points of nature, culture, and social relations. While in one sense modernity greatly heightens human interdependence, at the same time it sharply reduces our contact with others and with nature to the very narrow points of labor and commodities. It renders the rest of other peoples' lives largely invisible to us, as it does ours to them. We are workers and consumers together but little more.

So dense a conclusion requires step-by-step explanation.

The explanation begins with Borgmann's thesis that modern technology is not open at all—it is not an ensemble of waiting tools—but has a distinctive, consistent pattern, the device paradigm. The pattern's prime feature is a division and correlation of means and ends, of machinery and commodity, production and consumption, labor and leisure, the public and the private.[1] Understanding this requires lifting the edge of the tent to view the characteristics of the device paradigm itself.

In this paradigm, "devices" (machinery and the means of produc-

[1]Albert Borgmann, "Communities of Celebration: Technology and Public Life" in *Research in Philosophy and Technology: Technology and Religion*, ed. Frederick Ferré (Greenwich, Conn., and London: JAI Press, 1990), 10:335.

tion) constitute what Borgmann calls the background of technology, while "commodities" (both goods and services) constitute the foreground.

Background and foreground signal the paradigm's relationship of means and ends, machinery and commodities. The devices are there for the commodities. They serve no other purpose. Furthermore the devices largely recede from public view. Singularity of purpose and out-of-sight existence are major features of the means of production in the culture of modern technology. As for modern commodities, they are prized to the degree they are truly "commodious," that is, available without the encumbrance of means. Commodities at their best, in other words, are at our disposal without burdening us in any way. "Disburdenment" (Borgmann's word) is in fact a key element of the liberation vision of modernity itself, and its most common form is a fabulous array of available commodities that make life easier, more enjoyable, convenient, open to enriching choice, less burdensome.

So, for example, a central heating plant is a modern technological device, but a fireplace is not. Central heating provides the one thing it was devised for and nothing else—warm air. It requires nothing more of us than screwing the dial clockwise or counterclockwise to the temperature desired. We need not be familiar with how it works, much less truly understand it. We need ask no one for assistance or consult anyone in any way except perhaps to ask whether they are comfortable. No skills, no strength, no experience are needed. Furthermore we are not bothered by the unsightly presence of the machinery, nor do we know or much care where the compact metallic unit and ducting came from. (Georgia? Taiwan? Michigan? It doesn't matter.) We are not much concerned either about the people who made it and their lives, or how it got from their lives to ours. Not that we are insensitive. Not at all. Rather we have the "commodius" warm air as the sole purpose of the device, which is itself out of sight. The only element present, the only one intended to be present, is the pleasant air. Someone else's labor and goods, far in the background, and the commodity in our immediate presence—this, together with perhaps the six o'clock news, is our primary experience of the world of others.

A living-room or kitchen fireplace also provides warmth. It does so less efficiently and less comfortably than the central heating system. It is, in any event, far different from a modern "device." For one thing it is "burdensome," while central heating is not. Someone must cut and gather the wood, someone light and tend the fire, someone keep an eye on the firebox to make sure it stays filled, someone warm some hot chocolate or heat soup or make popcorn, someone take out the ashes and sweep the firebrick, someone now and again clean the chimney and check the flue, someone scout out the newly available fuel from a windstorm, trim the broken branches, and seed a new growth of trees.

What comes with this common routine is what Borgmann calls manifold engagement. Manifold engagement involves the practice of skills, the development of a discipline and fidelity to it, the broadening of sensibility, the profound interaction of human beings, and the development and preservation of tradition.[2] The fireplace is not just machinery and warmth. It is also a focus, a hearth, a place that gathers the members of the household from work and leisure, a location that gives the home a center. It engages its members. Duties are assigned, and, with it, responsibility is learned. Tasks are appointed, and, with them, skills are acquired. Conversation is carried on, as is working together and enjoying one another's company. With all of these, character is formed and subtly shaped. The fireplace, it is not too much too say, has communal moral dimensions, the upshot and outcome of its human engagement. The central heating system, by contrast, entails a simple, rather abstract action. It does not involve manifold engagement in the least.

Parallel contrast can be drawn between a TV dinner and the elaborate steps of preparing a meal together. The TV dinner is more "modern," measured by the device paradigm. It provides in unencumbered fashion what it as a commodity is for, in this case, a means for replenishing the body with food. As a modern commodity, it does not burden us. We receive nourishment and maintain health without needing any more direct assistance than a store clerk and a microwave oven. We need know nothing about food preparation beyond the instructions on the box. We need not know, and do not much care, who grew the vegetables or raised the cattle. We need not know nor care where this took place or how the food was processed and transported. We need not engage any of the very many persons on whom we have literally depended for this our daily bread. Our relationship to them is strictly commercial, strictly instrumental, and completely out of sight.

The difference from preparing the meal ourselves, with others, is marked. We might have grown some of the food. We planted the seeds or fed the lambs and enjoyed watching them grow, just as we enjoyed the sun and fresh air or were chilled and irritated by a cold mist. We were upset

[2]Albert Borgmann, *Technology and the Character of Contemporary Life* (Chicago and London: University of Chicago Press, 1984), 214.

about losing tomatoes to the blight and a lamb to an unknown malady. We likely did not prepare the meal wholly alone any more than we grew it, harvested it, cleaned it, and preserved it alone. We prepared it in the company of at least an other, if not several others. And we ate it, not to the six o'clock news and "Entertainment Tonight," as befits the TV dinner, but to the steady conversation of people around a table, the table itself now the focus of the home and the place of companionship. The meal itself has a structure, a liturgy, a sequence, some of it rich, some of it pedestrian, even occasionally boring.

Rich or not, this is more than consumption for nourishment's sake as the only end. It is what Borgmann calls a "focal practice,"[3] manifold engagement in a routine that itself becomes a vital part of a way of life and that cuts counter to the deadening, distancing power of the device paradigm. As a focal practice, the meal is certainly more than labor and commodities. It has a centering and orienting force and is the stuff of moral community. Escalating, it may even touch the sacred and partake of the sacramental, as when it becomes the Supper of the Lamb or Babette's feast. A TV dinner can be a convenient commodity, but it cannot be the bread of life itself. With the TV dinner something is present—abstract consumption—and something is absent, the rich world from which it has been abstracted. That world was lost in the process and the packaging.

The last example is water. The liberation vision of modern technology is that we need not toil or be burdened to meet our most basic needs. So we have safe, clean water by simply turning on the faucet at the kitchen sink or in the bathroom. Nothing more is required and nothing more happens, in keeping with the commodity up front and the device in recession as background.

A biblical allusion to Rebecca at the well is instructive. Borgmann, citing Daniel Boorstin, says that Rebecca, going to the well, found not only water but also companionship, news of the village, and her fiancé. "These strands of her life were woven into a fabric technology has divided and privatized into commodities."[4] This is no argument for women as virtual property, as Rebecca, or the hardship and confinement of village life, any more than the previous example assumed that women returning from out-of-home jobs were the sole preparers of the family meal. But Rebecca is an important contrast with, say, a woman standing

[3]Ibid., 196.
[4]Ibid., 119.

alone at the sink on the eleventh floor in a New York City studio apartment. What Borgmann calls "the presence of things"—Rebecca's community at the well—is replaced with the availability of commodities abstracted from everything in the world of their origins. Furthermore these commodities are made available by devices that themselves "dissolve the coherent and engaging character of the pretechnological world of things."[5] The relatedness of the world is replaced by the machinery (the fireplace and its ambience by the central heating system, the well and its social life by the apartment faucet). And the commodities are enjoyed "without the encumbrance of or the engagement with a context."[6]

Uncovering the paradigm further is less important at this juncture than noticing consequences. Living by this paradigm, with its narrow points of labor and commodities as the places we ourselves engage the world, means that we largely lose the more common reference points of nature, culture, and social relations. The commodities do not disclose the people who produced and supplied them, the region or place, the texture of their culture and way of life. We may depend on people close by and distant in ways earlier worlds never did, but we have no contact with them except the narrow one of personal use. Manifold engagement with those who provide for us is gone. If we think of them at all, our concern for these nameless, faceless ones is reduced to a worry that they continue to supply our wants.

At the same time, the vast availability of ends gives us the impression we are always making and remaking our own world, the engorging of life-styles we shall soon discuss.[7] We are told we are in control (consumer sovereignty), and we have the impression we are, income permitting.

Borgmann puts an ad and a cartoon side by side to show how, on the one hand, context—time, place, people—has been dissolved; and, on the other, how we entertain the illusion of manipulating the world we enjoy. The cartoon shows a buyer in front of a chest of frozen dinners, saying to her spouse, "For the big day, Harv, which do you want? The traditional American Christmas turkey dinner with mashed potatoes, giblet gravy, oyster dressing, cranberry sauce and tiny green peas or the old English Christmas goose dinner with chestnut stuffing, boiled potatoes, brussels

[5]Ibid., 47.

[6]Ibid.

[7]This is cited and discussed in the subsequent section.

sprouts and plum pudding?[8] The ad used for comparison is headed "We've just brought a world of good eating a lot closer." That world consists of beef chop suey with rice, Swedish meatballs in gravy with parsley noodles, linguini with clam sauce, chicken paprikash with egg noodles, chicken cacciatore with spaghetti, and beef teriyaki with rice and vegetables. This world has no depth or context. We are invited to feast Swedish style without contact with Sweden or Swedes, to enjoy Chinese without rubbing up against teeming Shanghai or Hong Kong. In the cartoon we are invited, as Borgmann says, not to "the world of bountiful harvests, careful preparations, and festive meals" but to a choice on December 25 about which "aggregate of commodities to consume."[9]

In a most insightful observation, Borgmann goes on to define consumption itself: "To consume is to use up an isolated entity without preparation, resonance, and consequence."[10] For our purposes, then, real Swedes, Chinese, and Italians don't matter. We enjoy them, or items attached to them, "without preparation, resonance, and consequence." It actually does not matter, either, whether English plum pudding is made in England, kinte cloth in Ghana, or Japanese cars in Japan. What matters is the utter end point, the commodity. Fulfillment is in its use, not in any of the worlds that have receded in the course of bringing it to us. They exist only as unreliable advertisements. For this reason, "technology upsets the tradition from the ground up."[11] All the relatedness to the pretechnological world is lost. Context is, at best, only cerebrally noted (made in Brazil, English plum pudding).

If we add Borgmann's discussion to what has gone before, we can now understand his complex conclusion. The promise of technology (liberation, enrichment, and the conquest of scourges that long assailed humanity) has led to the irony of technology. The irony is "when liberation by disburdenment yields to disengagement [from most every context], enrichment by way of diversion is overtaken by distraction, and conquest makes way first to domination and then to loneliness."[12] It is

---

[8]Cited in Borgmann, *Technology*, 51.
[9]Ibid.
[10]Ibid.
[11]Ibid., 46.
[12]Ibid., 76. "Conquest [making its way] first to domination" was discussed ear-

understandable, even from this short exposition, why Borgmann would go on to say that while technology does seem to be in accord with the liberal democratic values of liberty and equality (technology is no respecter of persons) and of self-realization (the expanded exercise of individual choices), it destroys the very community these values were to join as the moral triad of modernity. He does not mean that all technology does so—the ax that chops the wood for the hearth does not do so, nor the shovel that digs the hole for the new tree. He means technology working the grammar of the device paradigm. Nor does it destroy all conceivable community any more than the second bourgeois revolution does. But, like that revolution, it steadily wears away at life communities other than the "communities" of "mindless labor" and "distracting consumption."[13]

Furthermore, now agreeing with Boorstin, Borgmann says technology changes the meaning of liberty and equality's democracy itself, from a political system of collective self-rule to "a set of institutions which . . . aim to make everything available to everybody."[14] Advertising becomes "the characteristic rhetoric of democracy," Boorstin comments,[15] and people use democratic institutions as the means by which to press the good life understood as maximum consumer choice.

We can add a point made elsewhere, in Joel Kovel's *History and Spirit*. The workings of technology in this way "despiritualizes" the world. It doesn't kill the spirit—Kovel thinks that impossible—but represses it. More precisely, it "frees" people to pursue whatever spirituality they wish. And in the modern technological and capitalist order, they do so. But that matters not at all to the order of things itself. In the order of things, the economic and technological patterns deaden nature and issue in the utterly secular, resulting in the loss of the sacred at the heart of everyday experiences, not least in our work. This paradigm breaks up organic wholes into fragments and community into bits. Like Borgmann, Kovel does not count himself a Luddite. He does not rail against technology per se (whatever such an abstraction might mean). Nor does he consider modernity as such evil (Borgmann doesn't either). Kovel knows we

---

lier as Bacon's program of human control. "Then to loneliness" will be shown soon in the analysis done by Philip Slater.

[13]Ibid., 158.

[14]Ibid., 52.

[15]Ibid.

need different technologies and social patterns, working with rather than against nature and the human spirit. Such technologies are possible. Some already exist. The issue, however, is concrete; namely, the specific, pervasive playing out of the device paradigm as one of modernity's characteristic, though not inevitable, present features.[16]

The specific point we most want to underscore is the perverse outcome of all this for moral agency and community. The causes seem benign enough, quite in keeping with the basic assumptions of modernity. So conservatives and liberals alike are committed to a policy of economic growth and increased productivity, making the very best of the efficiencies, not to say the marvels, of modern technology. Yet pursuing this on the device paradigm has increased alienation and the degradation of work at the same time that it has promoted the fetishism of commodities. The workplace is not a happier, more fulfilling one in this scheme. Labor is fitted to the machine and role, not the other way around. Value is detached from human activity and attached to things.

Yet the rhetoric, echoing modernity's promise, boasts of high participation, personal agency, enhanced choice, and fulfillment. In the name of the paradigm, but against its actual workings, people talk of the "wholeness" just beyond their grasp and the opportunities for individual creativity that modernity and its technological marvels offer.

Nor is private life markedly better than the workplace. There is supposedly more leisure, yet it manifestly does not seem so.[17] The family, to mention one impacted community, has become more and more a setting for consumption and less and less the place where one generation initiates the next into a way of life in which all have a significant place and day-by-day participation. (In different words, the family is less and less the

---

[16]See Joel Kovel, *History and Spirit: An Inquiry into the Philosophy of Liberation* (Boston: Beacon Press, 1991), esp. the introduction, 1–16.

[17]There may in fact not be more leisure. Juliet B. Schor argues this in *The Overworked American: The Unexpected Decline of Leisure* (New York: Basic Books, 1992). Economic tightening and more members of the family in the work force mean longer work weeks, she says, and thus less leisure time. Moreover the nature of leisure-time activity has changed. People are more tired and prefer less active leisure—hanging out at the mall, vegging in front of the TV. More active leisure—participating in community and church events, learning to play a musical instrument, taking up a sport—is less attractive when the time for it actually comes. The result only increases the passivity and lowered sense of self we discussed in conjunction with the device paradigm.

most common locus of manifold engagement.) Thus while the promise was fulfillment, more and more families have to cope with emptiness and together search for significant bonds by which to tie members together as the single most essential human community. Exactly the wrong answer, of course, is to revive a romantic notion of *Kinder, Kirche, und Küche*, as conservatives are wont to do. It is wrong because the forces maiming family life are the very economic and technological ones conservatives largely support.

In a word, there is a loss of engagement and the experience of things in their own right in their many dimensions. Value is lifted from human activity together and attached to objects to be sold and used. The outcome is the paradox of apparently heightened choice, on the one hand, and the sense of powerlessness, ennui, and fragmentation, on the other. Moral agency, and the sense of responsibility and accountability that comes with meaningful participation, ebbs away, as community belonging does, together with compassion itself and the life of the spirit. Yet few challenge the technological paradigm, and certainly not improved productivity and greater consumption! Instead we respond to "high tech" with "high touch." But it is response to a lack, an effort to fill a void, rather than the promised gift of technological society itself. It is the intuitive quest for the kind of community that is being undermined by the logic we live. That kind of community is one of focal practices where the sacred is not absent nor nature deadened, and the organic whole is not broken into community bits.

Borgmann's description may leave little more to be said about the shape of modern technological society and its consequences for moral agency. We may have lost the immediacy of other aspects of our context in the process, however. More needs to be said about the condition of the people mentioned at the outset—middle America.

Catechisms

WHAT IS THE ETHOS AND WAY OF LIFE OF MIDDLE AMERICA NOW, AS full-fledged members of the technological society and modernity overall? Were its moral pulse charted, what vital signs would register? What kind of home does the device paradigm inhabit?

A decade ago I read Daniel Bell's *Cultural Contradictions of Capitalism.* It was an epiphany book. When Bell described modern culture and its moral ethos, I knew he was holding up to the light an X ray of white, middle-strata psyches and society. In two frames he outlined what Robert Bellah and his communion of research saints would document all over again twenty years later in *Habits of the Heart*. Bell wrote:

> Modern culture is defined by this extraordinary freedom to ransack the world storehouse and to engorge any and every style it comes upon. Such freedom comes from the fact that the axial principle of modern culture is the expression and remaking of the "self" in order to achieve self-realization and self-fulfillment. And in its search, there is a denial of any limits or boundaries to experience. It is a reaching out for all experience; nothing is forbidden, all is to be explored.
>
> Within this framework, one can discern the structural sources of tension in this society; between a social structure (primarily techno-economic) which is bureaucratic and hierarchical, and a polity which believes, formally, in equality and participation; between a social structure that is organized fundamentally in terms of roles and specialization, and a culture which is concerned with the enhancement and fulfillment of the self and the "whole" person. In these contradictions, one perceives many of the latent social conflicts that have been expressed ideologically as alienation, depersonalization, the attack on authority, and the like. In these adversary relations, one sees the disjunction of realms.[18]

Here is the standing American tradition of self-effected self-fulfillment as facilitated by an economic process potentially without limit. (Here is also confirmation of Borgmann's analysis.) The conviction is that we are essentially on our own, and society is a scene of exchange relations where all things—goods, labor, services, ideas, even relationships—are assembled, transformed, and traded. Moneyed and other contractual relationships begin, bless, gnarl, and terminate almost all relationships, and we "shop around" for everything—the right church, the right community, a good "pre-nup" agreement, the right divorce lawyer, clothes and cars that make a statement, classy Saladshooters and

[18]Daniel Bell, *The Cultural Contradictions of Capitalism* (New York: Basic Books, 1976), 13–14. My appreciation for Bell does not eliminate some fundamental disagreement. I do not accept the separation of politics, economics, and culture he posits, nor find the market nearly so benign as a moral force.

camcorders. The world is a "storehouse," and "freedom" is the freedom of the self fulfilling itself on the go, a "portable self"[19] in a malleable world. It is also a homeless self and, for all its incantations of freedom, an anxious, stressed one. Or so it would seem, since 5 percent of the world's population, living in a society of historically unprecedented affluence, uses 50 percent of the world's drugs and spends $160 billion annually—far more than the gross national product of most nations—on the diversions of entertainment, much of it prepackaged and patently idiotic, erupting into clear cases of "creeping nincompoopism."[20] And what is the preoccupation with stress, addiction, and codependency if not an accurate barometric reading of unsettled weather in a troubled self and soul?

Catechisms are to impart elementary wisdom, the kind we use time and again as rudder and guide. So if we ask what the moral temper of this society is, the middle-class child's cultural catechism is instructive evidence. Especially if the child is white and male, the internalized passage runs like this: Gather to yourself all you can—experience, knowledge, goods, skills. Make your own world, as you see fit, and enjoy. Grow for all your worth, in every way. Never close off any options. "Nothing is forbidden, all is to be explored" (Bell). Not heard is a catechism common to many long-standing religious traditions and many minority peoples, as well as others who have had to stare down heavy odds year in and year out: You will find yourself with needs that cannot be satisfied and wants that cannot be fulfilled. There are circumstances beyond your control and fears not easily appeased. So learn courage, endurance, sacrifice, and patience. Recognize powers beyond your own, and accept the world with joy.

All this and more the authors of *Habits of the Heart* documented in their discussion of individualism among white Americans. In *The Good Society*, the authors move from this moral, spiritual, and psychic impoverishment into their proposal for a more communitarian democracy focused on revitalizing our patterned ways of living together (their definition of institutions). We will also visualize the church as a commu-

[19]From James T. Yenckel's interview with Robert C. Weigl, "Private Lives: The Portable Self," in *Washington Post*, 9 April 1980, B5.

[20]The statistics are from Bellah et al., *The Good Society* (New York: Alfred A. Knopf, 1991), 4. The reference to "creeping nincompoopism" is from a review by Christopher Buckley of Paul Fussell's *Bad* in *New York Times Book Review*, 13 October 1991, sect. 7, p. 9.

nity of moral conviction by focusing on moral renewal via the practices of a concrete way of life. Yet this is to run ahead of the story. A glimpse at the 1980s is a necessary chapter. We should be prepared for those ironies history seems diabolically to enjoy collecting.

The 1980s

THE 1980S ARE IRRESISTIBLE TO MORAL ANALYSIS BECAUSE THE CHIEF movement of the decade, that of conservatives and neoconservatives, explicitly used a moral vocabulary. In fact the newfound power of the merged political and religious right was nothing less than a full moral crusade. "Traditional values," or "Judeo-Christian values," sometimes "family values," were invoked in an effort to restore moral order and collective public purpose to a nation suffering "malaise."

Yet by decade's end it was clear that "spiritual disrepair" was as evident as it was in the 1970s. "The slide into apathy, hedonism, and moral chaos" had not been halted in the least.[21] On the contrary, the social fabric continued to unravel during the Reagan years, and the "unbridled pursuit of worldly success,"[22] with little concern for neighbor, the public welfare, or future generations, continued unabated. Together with a "baffled sense of drift,"[23] the disrepair continues in the 1990s as the high costs of the 1980s take their toll and the bills are delivered to the next generation, increasingly a disillusioned and demoralized one. Since this seemed so contrary to the moral intentions and the tone of public rhetoric, we must rewind the tape to see what actually happened.

As noted, the appeal was to "traditional values." Traditional values have usually meant those values of the bourgeois revolution and the Protestant ethic important to the initial establishment of democratic capitalism—thrift, honesty, self-denial, frugality, hard work, discipline, deferred gratification, avoidance of all wastefulness, and marital, family, and community fidelity and loyalty. They have also meant a distinction between a domestic, or private, sphere and a public one. The former, chiefly through home, school, and church as led by women's energies and sensibilities, was to effect those virtues that the market of itself did

[21]Christopher Lasch, *The True and Only Heaven: Progress and Its Critics* (New York: W. W. Norton, 1991), 22.
[22]Ibid.
[23]Ibid.

not promote or sustain. A kinder and gentler morality would thereby civilize or humanize largely male-dominated public life. While "traditional values" remained the working vocabulary of the Bush-Quayle years, and while the public versus private distinction had nostalgic echoes even of the 1950s, any comparison with the values actually promoted by acquisitive individualism and unlimited growth wasn't even within hailing distance of conservatism's traditional values. Any comparison with boosterism and consumerism and the hedonistic gratifications used as nonstop titillation by corporate advertising; any comparison with the promotion of unbounded appetites, unlimited opportunities, and maximally deregulated freedom; any comparison with life as a series of styles to be explored without restraint or lasting obligation; any comparison of this entire moral set with "traditional values" makes it very clear that these values, like tradition itself, were simply undermined, even scorned, in the 1980s.

What was promoted was not traditional moral conservatism at all, with its attachment to time, place, history, memory, and the responsibility that attends preserving a legacy. Instead the aggressive, male-minded personality was promoted, a personality not tied down anywhere to anyone, including home and family, a personality with unlimited freedom to make and remake the world according to his or her desires in a freewheeling market. Nor was the sober voice of traditional conservative wisdom ever promoted, with its sense of limits and the need to sacrifice. On the contrary, talk of limits and binding obligations were the "counsels of doom" of "naysayers," to cite candidate Reagan's words used to chide President Carter and others guilty of spreading "malaise." Traditional conservatism's sense of historical continuity was not promoted, either, and certainly not its feel for the persistence of subtle collective sinfulness, especially sinfulness as the self-deception and illusion to which collective pride and power are prone. Instead "morning in America" had dawned in full innocence and righteousness, and history had turned a sure corner. The new day was itself broadly welcomed by the national psyche, especially among white men of all socioeconomic strata. It was powerfully augmented by President Reagan's sense for the mystic chords of patriotism and his talent for selling used cars, or most anything.

Traditional conservative "pay-as-you-go" economics was totally out of favor in the 1980s, even though it belonged to the core way of life associated with traditional values. The most essential conservative value of all, prudence, was completely absent. So instead of prudent pay-as-you-go economics and social policy, the much ballyhooed "largest continuous economic expansion in history" was financed by the largest debt expansion in history. (The gross federal debt moved from $1 trillion in 1981, after 205 years of U.S. history, to $4.08 trillion in 1992, with a projection of $4.5 trillion by the end of fiscal 1993, thus more than quadrupling in slightly more than a decade.[24] As a percentage of GNP, it increased 200 percent in the Reagan-Bush years.[25] This left us the largest debtor nation in the world, measured in sheer dollar amount, and with federal interest payments as the third largest category of spending in the national budget, trailing only Social Security and military expenditures. Debt interest alone in 1992 hit $293 billion.[26] And this after Reagan-Bush shifted many social expenditures to states and cities!)[27] Debt expansion, though not economic growth, continued with new record deficits in each of the Bush-Quayle years. (The 1991 actual deficit, itself a record, was $269 billion. The 1992 deficit was still more—$290 billion, adding further to an already runaway debt.)[28]

The cautious personality of traditional conservatism, concerned with moral rectitude and propriety, was nowhere to be found in the 1980s. Insofar as any one comment can capture the general tone of the decade, it was best expressed by President Reagan himself at a press conference in 1983: "What I want to see above all is that this country remains a country where someone can always get rich. That's the one thing we have and that must be preserved."[29] As if to make the point dramatically, American chief executive officers (CEOs) received 160 times the earnings of average workers in the 1980s. They still do, thereby carefully protecting the robber baron traditions of industry and finance. Some of them rake in far more, even though this looting of America never receives the reproach

---

[24]"The Crucial Issue Politicians Ignore," *New York Times*, 24 April 1992, D2.

[25]The figures are from David A. Stockman, "Hands off the Economy," *New York Times*, 27 January 1992, A21.

[26]"The Crucial Issue Politicians Ignore," *New York Times*, 24 April 1992, D2.

[27]"Economy Likely to Revive Soon, Congress Is Told," *New York Times*, 22 January 1992, A13.

[28]"Clinton's Bright Ideas Get to Meet the Ugly Facts," *New York Times*, 10 January 1993, sect. 4, p. 1.

[29]Quoted in Bellah, et al., *The Good Society*, 87. Bellah et al. have reported Reagan's press conference remark from Jennifer L. Hochschild, "The Double-Edged Sword of Equal Opportunity," in *Power, Inequality, and Democratic Politics: Essays in Honor of Robert A. Dahl*, ed. Ian Shapiro and Grant Recher (Boulder and London: Westview Press, 1988), 168.

of, say, the Los Angeles riots. The estimated average 1990 annual salary and other compensation of the thirty largest U.S. companies' CEOs was $3.4 million. (The comparable figure for Germans was $800,000 and Japanese $500,000.) Hardly content with averages, Steven J. Ross and N. J. Nicholas, Jr. of Time Warner received $99.6 million between them; Paul B. Fireman of Reebok International $33.3 million; Rand Araskog of ITT $11.5 million and U.S. Surgical's Leon C. Hirsch $15 million. Top prize, however, went to Roberto C. Goizueta of Coca-Cola, who received either $63.5 million or about $81.4 million in total 1991 compensation, depending on when the value of the million shares of stock he received was calculated.[30]

In the failing automobile empires, Lee Iacocca of Chrysler, a popular figure and something of a corporate guru, was paid $4.65 million in 1990 and given $718,000 in Chrysler shares. Chrysler, having been bailed out under Reagan and in turn providing help to the deserving needy, bought two of Iacocca's houses when he failed to get his asking price in the depressed real estate market. General Motors' chairman, Robert Stempel, while announcing massive layoffs and the sharp "downsizing" of GM, was receiving $2.18 million in compensation. His predecessor, Roger Smith, receives an annual retirement pension of $1 million. The twenty-one American CEOs who accompanied President Bush to Japan in 1992 made on average $2 million annually in salary alone (not total compensation), while their Japanese counterparts, hardly the business world's paupers, received one-sixth that figure and customarily pay taxes at 65 percent of income.[31] Unlike the Japanese in another way, none of the U.S. executives had salaries indexed to the profitability of the companies they headed. Moreover CEO compensation in the U.S. increased 275 percent between 1980 and 1990, while the compensation of hourly workers increased 60 percent and corporate profits 10 percent.[32]

CEOs weren't alone in meeting Reagan's hope for America. The

---

[30]"Coke's Chief Paid a Million Shares in '91," *New York Times*, 19 March 1992, D1.

[31]Anthony Lewis, "Metaphor for Failure," *New York Times*, 5 January 1992, E13. Lewis is drawing from a *Wall Street Journal* article by Jill Abramson and Christopher J. Chipello. There is an error in his account. He lists the CEOs with President Bush as twelve, but there were twenty-one. The data used by Lewis is verified in a feature article drawing on other sources. See "The Gadfly C.E.O.'s Want to Swat," *New York Times*, 2 February 1992, sect. 3, p. 1.

[32]"The Gadfly C.E.O.'s Want to Swat," ibid., p. 6.

1980s saw a dramatic escalation of wealth for the already rich. The top 1 percent of U.S. families garnered 60 percent of the growth in after-tax income between 1977 and 1989 and 77 percent of pretax income. People in the middle (i.e., the median) saw their income edge up 4 percent in the same period while the bottom 40 percent of families actually experienced declines in these "boom" years. They were boom years because productivity increased and more people joined the work force, not because the majority was better off as measured by buying power or share in the national income. The 1989 average pretax income for the top 1 percent was $559,800 and the top 20 percent $109,400, while the bottom 20 percent averaged $8,400 and the middle 60 percent ran the range from $20,100 to $47,900.[33] The figures for wealth, as contrasted with income, were even more dramatic. In 1983 the richest 1 percent of American families owned 31 percent of the nation's wealth, while the bottom 90 percent owned 33 percent. By 1989 the richest 1 percent owned 37 percent while the bottom 90 percent owned 32 percent. Lest that not be fully clear, it means that combined, 834,000 households were worth more than 84,000,000 households ($5.7 trillion to $4.8) and it means that the gap in wealth distribution was growing.[34] To cap it all off, the ranks of the poor—14.2 percent of the population—were higher in 1991 (35.7 million) than any year since 1964.[35]

At the same time the wealth escalated among a diminished portion of the population, charitable giving actually declined as a percentage of income. In 1979 people who made more than $1 million (as measured in constant 1991 dollars) gave somewhat over 7 percent of after-tax income to charity. It reached a highpoint in 1981 when it hit 10 percent. Thereafter it dropped so that over the next ten years it ended up by 1991 at less than 4 percent.[36]

Given this vocation for America (getting rich as "the one thing we have . . . that must be preserved") and the moral substance of this way of life, it is classic irony that Reagan and the right, who live as far from the Protestant

---

[33]"The 1980's: A Very Good Time for the Very Rich," *New York Times*, 5 March 1992, A1. The source of data is the Congressional Budget Office.
[34]"Fed Gives New Evidence of 80's Gains by Richest," *New York Times*, 21 April 1992, A1.
[35]"Ranks of U.S. Poor Reach 35.7 million, the most since '64," *New York Times*, 4 September 1992, A1.
[36]"Charitable Gifts by the Rich Are up, But on Average They're Giving Less," *New York Times*, 24 May 1992, L16.

ethic and traditional values as anyone can get and still be on the same planet, should decry "permissiveness" and moral relativism or should make claims to moral conservatism as their ethic. Permissiveness is the true moral expression of the economic culture they, together with millions of others, promoted and still promote. Our economic culture lives by the notion of the world as a storehouse to be ransacked for the good life, understood as maximum personal pleasure. It flourishes with the endless pursuit of new methods of self-indulgence. It thrives on novelty, change, excitement, possession, and the titillation of the senses with every conceivable stimulant.[37] It makes every effort to create new markets. Its engines propel themselves by new demands, the creation of new discontents and a never-ending supply of new toys, drugs, and services. Relativism of tastes and a lifetime of changing tastes is what the economy strives for and counts on. Far from confirming traditional values, this culture erodes tradition and uproots settled, close communities. Furthermore, as Lasch points out, the model of possession in a society organized around mass consumption, as ours is, is addiction. The "need for novelty and fresh stimulation becomes more and more intense" while "intervening interludes of boredom [become] increasingly intolerable."[38] "Shop 'til you drop" and a trip to one of the thirty thousand malls is a kind of hit, then; or if that is offensive, a therapy session. (One survey of mall shoppers reported that only 25 percent came to buy a particular item.)[39] For conservatives, neoconservatives, and the religious right to rail against hedonism, permissiveness, and moral relativism while energetically supporting the economic culture of the 1980s and its expression in the mass media is an irony worthy of a Far Side cartoon in which blindspots are framed and hung on the wall as captivating art, or the seven deadly sins—greed, avarice, envy, gluttony, luxury, and so on—are lavishly dressed out as virtues worn by cows and paraded in a fashion show before a wildly enthusiastic audience of livestock.

Where has this left us? It is certainly clear that the morality of the 1980s abandoned the traditional bourgeois ethic, which, with its restraint, was an ethic tailored to savings, investment, and production. It passed over to an ethic of narcissism, which, with its abandon, is an ethic of consumption. Furthermore the society took on market logic and ways well beyond the market itself, embracing the second bourgeois revolu-

---

[37]Lasch, *The True and Only Heaven*, 520.
[38]Ibid., 520–21.
[39]Ibid., 521.

tion. Citizens became chiefly clients, customers, and consumers in a joyless economy carefully skewed to further favor the already rich.

The moral ethos here went far beyond an ethic for economic life only. Celebrities replaced heroes and heroines, and moral models worthy of the name hardly existed at all (Lee Iacocca? Oliver North? Madonna? Jerry Falwell? Nancy Reagan? Donald Trump?). Self-help was substituted for any religion that might ask for discipleship. Psychobabble and "talking it out" in endlessly created artificial environments substituted for conversation and community.[40]

We are left, then, with tiny lives whose idea of the Spirit is as an aid to help fix, manage, and control a world of our own crafting. There is no genuine transcendent referent here, no cosmic meaning or larger significance beyond the self. De Tocqueville's observations of more than 150 years ago reappeared with new validity: "Each citizen is habitually busy with the contemplation of a very petty object, which is himself"; and "there is a danger [each citizen] may be shut up in the solitude of his own heart."[41]

In a word, the morality promoted by recent culture is a solipsistic closed circuit of acquisitive and therapeutic individualism fueled by corporate economic dynamics and maximally deregulated freedom understood as raw liberty. Whatever its achievements along the way, living its moral convictions gradually destroys worlds. It does so in the name and hope of progress but leaves us with a social and moral recession that will outlast any economic one.

Unfortunately the conventional moral analysis of the 1980s is of little help, even retrospectively. It laments the decade of greed while at the same time searching for ways to get the same economic growth back on track. Greed may be a genuine threat, though less as a matter of individual motivation and personal vice, despite the robber baron mentality, than as the expression of the institutionalized, systemic drive for markets and profits. At the very time Reagan dismantled sectors of the federal government in the name of decentralization, he promoted the consolidating and conglomerating of centers of economic power. Dampening the appetites, therefore—should anyone run on that unlikely platform—is

---

[40]Rohr, "Why Does Psychology Always Win?" *Sojourners* 19 (July 1990): 13–14.
[41]See the discussion by Alexis de Tocqueville, *Democracy in America*, trans. George Lawrence, ed. J. P. Mayer (New York: Doubleday, Anchor Books, 1969), 506–10.

hardly the path to a kinder, gentler morality when the culture of mass production and consumption is the economy's infrastructure itself. Dampening the appetites in fact remains the explicit public foe. Voices uniformly call for stronger "consumer confidence" and the getting and spending for which it is a euphemism.

Differently said, the 1980s chipped away at the second of the three prime democratic values, equality, while interpreting the remaining one, liberty, in a way that subordinated political decisions to economic ones. "The one thing we have . . . that must be preserved," to recall Reagan on America, is this country as one "where someone can always get rich." Democracy shrivels to "freedom of choice" as a consumer mentality and "interests" as the chief political expression. (Money spent on advertising actually now exceeds that expended for public schools, from kindergarten through high school.) Democracy is little more than the market and the ballot box.

The extent to which democracy in the U.S. is now a matter of market and ballot box, even market and ballot box together, was nicely illustrated by the White House spokesman Marlin Fitzwater during the 1992 presidential campaign. He was responding to questions about the "President's Dinner," a campaign fund-raiser in which people paid from $1,500 to $400,000 for the opportunity to mingle with President Bush, his staff, and the Republican members of Congress. (The dinner raised $8 million.) Asked whether the donors were buying access to President Bush's top aides, Fitzwater replied: "It's buying access to the system, yes. That's what the political parties and the political system is all about." Asked how less wealthy citizens could buy their way into the system, Fitzwater said: "They have to demand access in other ways."[42]

Still, a season of ostentatious greed and hedonism is not the worst of the damage. A laughable, even cynical, notion of equality, and a conception of liberty as freedom to ravage the world storehouse and engorge every style (to recall Bell), are worse. After all, no one claimed greed as an essential of the democratic creed. But liberty and equality are *sine qua non*. The peril escalates when community, that forgotten essential, is assessed and the damage to community moral formation is raised to full view. What the life orientation of the 1980s did not do, and could not,

[42]In raising this $8 million, $15,000 allowed one to sit with a Republican member of Congress, $92,000 got one a photo with the president. "Bush May Get Tab for G.O.P. Dinner," *New York Times*, 29 April 1992, A18.

with its solipsistic closed moral circuit, was create care for one another and the planet, or any other marks of healthy moral community. On the contrary, moral skills learned only in community, and their extension as a sense of public obligation beyond the boundaries of face-to-face encounters, were trampled by the morality of the 1980s, despite all the appeals to voluntarism, self-reliance, and charity as the works of citizenship. This destruction of moral community, already only tenuous at best in the modern world, was perhaps the worst effect of the '80s, outstripping even the economic hangover from rampant speculation, foolish mergers, irresponsible lending and borrowing, and silly "supply-side" government fiscal policy.

Moral community's degradation was so far advanced by the 1980s' life-style that we have almost forgotten the reason for democracy in the first place—to foster in people the capacity to direct their lives together intelligently and creatively within a safe and sustainable environment. The basic question of democracy is not the market and ballot box question, What do people want? at least not as a question without careful preparation. The question is not interests and how power can be organized, usually through money, to realize them. The first question is how people get to be what they want to be and how they get to want what it is they want. It is a moral question, a question of human character and capacity and their formation.

The profound reply to this question *is* democracy, but only when democracy provides for the health of civil communities; that is, only when liberty and equality mean reciprocal and participatory action with others in order to achieve common goals and develop personal agency. If freedom is no more than selecting items from a menu in order to use and consume them, then democracy is an empty hulk and community is virtually nonexistent.[43] Our abilities to develop responsibility and account-

---

[43]See the fine discussion by Samuel Bowles and Herbert Gintis, "The Economy Produces People: An Introduction to Post-Liberal Democracy," in *Religion and Economic Justice*, ed. Michael Zweig, (Philadelphia: Temple University Press, 1991), 221–44. An earlier chapter adds to the foregoing discussion above the reasons why liberalism failed to be a deterrent against neo-conservative and other right-wing advocates of the market. Michael Lerner, in "Jewish Liberation Theology and Emancipatory Politics," writes:

> Just as surely as capitalism tends to impoverish people materially, so it tends to drain us spiritually. In one of the great ironies of political life in the United States today, it is right-wing champions of the market and

ability are then arrested, and our capacities for social participation and critically informed choices are hardly developed at all, except perhaps as laborers and consumers in the manner of the device paradigm.

One last item finishes this analysis. More than two decades ago, sociologist Philip Slater investigated what he concluded was the unintended yet rather systematic pursuit of loneliness (also Borgmann's finding). The middle U.S. American household found it perfectly normal to seek a private means of transportation, a private laundry, and self-service stores. When economically feasible, the kids would get a separate room with a separate phone, stereo, perhaps TV, and, in the driveway, a separate car. The promise was more freedom, and the goal seemed to be a world of one's own making and control in which one did not have to ask a single other human being for help. The actual outcome was not privacy and fulfilling leisure so much as a vague loneliness, low-level depression, and a restless spirit. The solution? Find yet another gadget, fad, or experience, including religious experience, to make one's little world more precisely the way one wanted.[44] For Slater this was "American Culture at the Breaking Point" (the subtitle of his book).

All this should not be laid at the feet of recent U.S. capitalism alone. And that has not been the argument here. The argument, as intimated,

---

> classical liberal thought who have most clearly taken up the family crisis, the decline in public values, and the breakup of our communities. Unfairly, they have blamed these crises on the struggle for individual rights, claiming that these struggles (embodied in the civil rights movement and the movements of women and gays) have provided the pernicious individualism that undermines family and community. But as long as critics of capitalism fail to address the crisis in families and communities in a coherent way, fail to help people find a way to cope with the pain they feel in their daily lives, that pain will be manipulated by the right to justify its programs. The prospects for transforming society into a place of justice and human dignity will be all the more remote if the liberal and progressive forces fail to address the psychological and spiritual needs that are just as central to most people as their needs for economic security and political rights (140).

[44]See Philip Slater, *The Pursuit of Loneliness: American Culture at the Breaking Point* (Boston: Beacon Press, 1970). Bellah et al., in *The Good Society*, 62, recall an advertisement of General Motors that nicely illustrates what Slater found, but renders it positive. The advertisement makes a second car a virtue and, with a family barbecuing in front of two shiny new autos, declares: "Going Our Separate Ways We've Never Been So Close."

has been that the 1980s constitute the most recent installment of an evolving, dynamic investment in modernity that has led to diminishing moral and community fragments. The dynamics of unabashed consumer capitalism have been a substantial and corrosive part of this, to be sure, as has the notion of democracy hitched to the market on terms that demanded that we do nothing more than vote our own interests (Rancho San Diego). But so has our confidence that science and technology would let limitless possibilities issue from the conquest of the natural, social, and psychic worlds. A life without limits in a world of our own making was the dream and drive of modernity well before Reagan and well before the first neoconservative was invented; Promethean power for human conquest and economic messianism reach back to modernity's beginnings.

Yet the entire amalgam of modernity in its militantly white, male, and rich American form hit full stride with Reagan culture and Bush ethics. The episode was both tumultuous and curious, for just as central-command socialism, one of modernity's most confident and massive monuments, collapsed in on itself of its own dead weight, free wheeling democratic capitalism, modernity's other testimony to historical genius on a grand scale, banished all self-doubt whatsoever and jubilantly strode to center stage to announce its victory, even "the end of history" (Fukuyama). What the 1980s witnessed, then, was modernity's credo lived with new bourgeois vengeance and in such a way that basic moral formation of character and conscience was left to modernity's autonomous individuals, their markets, their minimalist state, and their unbounded appetites.[45] The result is that steady, intact communities of basic moral formation and manifold engagement hardly exist at all now in the U.S. For people who thought they were walking the edge of glory, awakening to the consequences is a cruel realization and the reason middle America in the 1990s is such demoralized terrain. The answer to Wolfe's question, "Can bourgeois society survive bourgeois man?" is still out.

[45]Bellah et al., *The Good Society*, 6.

CHAPTER 6

Everything at Once

Everything Is Too Much

THE POISONOUS SIDE OF MODERNITY HAS NOT ACCOMPLISHED ITS FULL end. We retain resilient fragments of morality and community. People still make long-term commitments to family and friends and shoulder the blessings and burdens of open-ended responsibility. People still relegate their own immediate interests to the well-being of others. They still join together in cooperative endeavors to fashion a better and more responsive society. Nonetheless we cannot deny the composite analysis of the foregoing chapters that leaves us with the solipsistic, postpublic morality of the 1980s and its market model for all things great and small; the transformation of community into transient enclaves of privacy; the erosion of civil society as the incubator and laboratory of public life and its requisite moral base; the necessary but deficient employ of society-as-market and society-as-state as primary moral proxies; the recourse to market and state as models of society itself and inadequate substitutes for the moral communities they have drawn on but neglected and lamed; and the pernicious reduction of human agency and imagination to mindless labor and distracting consumption as a way of life in "advanced" technological society. One could summarize in Gregory Baum's words: "Contemporary culture undermines all forms of social solidarity."[1]

With this as the unhappy state of affairs, and modernity itself thrash-

[1]Gregory Baum, "The State of the Council," *Christianity & Crisis* 49, 2/6 (1989): 11. I am grateful to Christian Iosso for bringing this to my attention.

ing about with postmodernity, community and the moral life stare at a demanding historical moment. We will tag it "everything at once." (Pogo's "insurmountable opportunities" comes to mind as the alternative.) It is a moment in which we must do basic moral formation, chiefly the character and conscience formation of persons and communities, at the same time that we address massive social problems and seek more viable institutions. We must do this with communities that have moral formation and soulcraft as their vocation (the family, religious and educational institutions in the first ranks) at the same time that we must care for and regenerate these reeling communities themselves, hunkered down as many are in a coping, even survivalist, mode. We must undertake cultural change alongside social and institutional change.

The moment is curious as well as demanding. The microcosmic unit of society, the family, continues in transition amid changing forms and experiences no little trouble just when we are called on to strengthen large societies. We hardly know how to preserve small families within society, much less create new bonds across society and across societies. At the very time when the distinctive character and culture of many local communities is eroding from the world of media and market that overwhelms them, we are called on to work together as solid citizens for a democratic world community, which is itself in the midst of wrenching political realignments and economic tumult. At a time when the moral breakdown of this society is reflected in the doubled prison population of the past decade, moving the United States into the ranks of those nations with the highest percentage of the population incarcerated (we have joined South Africa and the former U.S.S.R.), we are called on to trust one another more in a setting of increasing interdependence. At a time when we do too little to remember, appreciate, and preserve the hard-won contributions of the ancestors, we are called on to respect the needs of future generations in a world of advancing environmental degradation and a population that threatens to smother itself in its own numbers.[2]

At a time when the world experiences heightened interdependence and vulnerability on most every front, we seem to have fewer guidelines

---

[2]See the quite astonishing verse, 2 Bar. 23:3: "And [the Lord] answered and said to me . . . 'For just as you have not forgotten the people who now are, and those who have passed away, so I remember those who are to come.' " I am grateful to Thomas E. McCollough, *The Moral Imagination and Public Life*, (Chatham, N.J.: Chatham House Publishers, 1991), epigraph for chap. 1, for this citation.

for organizing our obligations toward one another. And the place in which we must create clear guidelines is confusion itself! We need people of character and a strong public morality as much as ever, yet we have too little sense of the common good or the institutional forms required for its promotion. Not least, we face moral education and a sense of moral centeredness as a requirement not just for children now, but adults as well, the very adults responsible for morally mentoring the next generation.

In short, we stand center stage at a curious modern-postmodern moment when we must respond to unprecedented moral demands—both basic character formation and a bewildering array of social problems—just when the moral codes and the communities that put flesh on them are exceptionally weak. This is a serious case of "insurmountible opportunities" and "everything at once."

Differently said, the intersection of modernity and postmodernity means that we are in for a long season of unavoidable experimentation. It is experimentation on a local, regional, national, and international scale in which the quest for viable institutions and policies happens at the same time that pressing issues of all kinds must themselves be addressed from a moral point of view. Morality itself is created and re-created in such times, and this is itself part of the groping experimentation.

If all this appears overwhelming, the reason is simple. It is. We live in an overwhelming moment. We must strengthen moral communities and replenish moral reservoirs even as we draw from them amid the "forced options" that times-between-times serve up without first knocking and asking permission to enter.[3]

For many, the spirit itself balks just as we embark on all this. Amid real exhilaration and hope, there suddenly appears a strong undertow of severe world-weariness, a long wash of low-pedal tones in the psyche, and a kind of exhaustion with life, at least life together on a noisy, overcrowded, saturated planet. Just when people thought, in the pattern typical of modernity, that they had taken control of their lives, they discover

[3]"Forced options" is a phrase from Roger Shinn, *Forced Options: Social Decisions of the Twenty-first Century* (Cleveland: Pilgrim Press, 1991). Shinn took the phrase from William James in his essay "The Will to Believe." There it means, now in Shinn's words, "a decision that allows no escape. Any efforts to delay it for long, to sit it out, to compromise indefinitely are themselves decisions—as surely as is the deliberate choice of one of the alternatives" (3).

life will not be controlled, or is itself out of control. Everything at once is too much.

Inappropriate Religion and Community

THE NEXT CHAPTERS TAKE UP THE CONSTRUCTIVE RESPONSE. MATTERS of the spirit as well as community's moral tasks are included. This chapter finishes by describing the inappropriate religious inclinations of modernity and postmodernity when our concern is the church as a constructive community of moral formation and conviction. We clear the way for the next chapters by rejecting some familiar choices.

The cultural style of modernity and the fragmentation of the postmodern spiritual search generates, in George Lindbeck's words, "multitudes of men and women who are impelled, if they have religious yearnings, to embark on their own individual quests for symbols of transcendence."[4] Furthermore the churches have largely become "conveyors of this commodity" (individually tailored quests for transcendence) "rather than communities that socialize their members into coherent and comprehensive religious outlooks and forms of life."[5] Religious groups are less communities of moral socialization into distinctive ways of life than they are, now in Catherine Albanese's phrase, "booth keepers in an emporium of transcendence."[6] What brought us to this role for the churches, Albanese explains, is the progressive weakening of moral communities combined with the increase of a therapeutic and individualistic orientation in the middle classes. Thus "ego boundaries" have become "more pronounced" in this century while community boundaries have faded.[7] This in turn means that churches and synagogues not only compete with any number of other organizations that confer meaning, advertise values, and try to grab people's attention for the tasks of living well, but the style is one suited to going it alone in religious matters and/or trafficking in transient communities—the rock concert, the sporting event, the never-miss TV series, the self-help or support group. For

---

[4] George Lindbeck, *The Nature of Doctrine: Religion and Theology in a Postliberal Age* (Philadelphia: Westminster Press, 1984), 126.

[5] Ibid.

[6] Catherine L. Albanese, "Forum," in *Religion and American Culture: A Journal of Interpretation* 1/2 (Summer 1991): 138.

[7] Ibid., 140.

much of this, the "clientele" (to use an archetypal modern word) privileges inner and even mystical states, is suspicious of organization, authority, and exclusive allegiances, prefers the oxymoron of "nonbinding commitments," and chooses religious fit and authenticity by judging how well it answers "personally identified life situations and experiences."[8]

All this is sufficiently privatized that often we do not know the religious and moral convictions of the people we rub up against all the livelong day. They may dress like us, share our funny accent, and chuckle at the same ethnic jokes, but we will not know whether they are Catholic charismatic, soft New Age, Buddhist, utterly secular humanist, deep ecologist, or pious Lutheran. And we will not find out until there is some casual or intimate setting and conversation in which they choose to share what they normally do not. Incidentally, we should not be surprised to find that much of this modern-postmodern religious style is characterized by low-cal or "lite" spirituality with the whiff of weekend workshops, the spark of low-voltage discipleship, and the glitzy packaging of ready-to-wear, one-size-fits-all faith.[9] Nor should we be surprised, amid postmodern quests and confusion, that religion is a ready collection point for a vast array of nebulous personal yearnings and a kind of dumpster for every sort of personal problem.

What does this religious style mean for the moral life? Robert Wuthnow's *Acts of Compassion: Caring for Others and Helping Ourselves* is important, if inadvertant, commentary on this. Wuthnow set out to discover what motivates people in nonmarket ways, that is, ways not explicitly appealing to their self-interest. He found that religious motivation per se was not a decisive motivator of other-regarding behavior. What counted was the degree of community or individualism associated with one's faith.[10] Wuthnow distinguishes "spirituality" from "religion" and is concerned that many people are, as Lindbeck and Albanese noted, pursuing their spirituality quite apart from any formal religious community. But the salient point is his finding that the decisive factor in whether or not caring activities occur is community. "Spirituality is conducive to caring activities only when it occurs within the context of such commu-

---

[8]Ibid., 141.

[9]Charlene Spretnak, *States of Grace: The Recovery of Meaning in the Postmodern Age* (San Francisco: HarperCollins, 1991), 28.

[10]Robert Wuthnow, *Caring for Others and Helping Ourselves* (Princeton: Princeton University Press, 1991), 153–56.

nities" (religious communities).[11] Privatized religion apparently dampens concern for others, while commitment to a community sets in motion those dynamics that draw us into the webs of association that bind us together, sensitize us to needs beyond our own, and call forth active response to and with others. Disturbingly, Wuthnow confirms a postmodern phenomenon among baby boomers. He found them to carry both a greater yearning for spirituality and a greater reluctance to commit to religious communities. (Part of this may, of course, be that in this economy two-career families have less time for community commitments of any kind.)

In conclusion, the moral state among white middle Americans is something like this: We can often speak eloquently of our needs, desires and feelings (thanks to expressive individualism, even some shy Lutherans are getting better at it by the day); but we lack utterly the language of moral formation, obligation, and public commitment. Why? Richard Rohr thinks it is because the therapeutic mentality has triumphed in such degree among middle Americans that there is no goal in our discourse "beyond the process itself or that elusive thing called healing, therapy, or recovery."[12] We crave intimacy itself as community but there is no ethic here beyond "listening." Nonjudgmental openness is prized, conflict and guilt are shunned. "Warmth is our god," Richard Sennett announced already in 1979 in *The Fall of Public Man.*[13] So while it is a mortal sin to repress any feelings, fears, or sexual fantasies, Rohr complains, it is totally acceptable to repress the objective issues of famine, destruction of habitat, and arms sales to everybody.[14] We could add urban squalor, racism, and any number of other everyday public perversions.

All this we met earlier among the white, middle-strata figures of *Habits of the Heart.* They had no grounds for moral commitments beyond self-referential ones, no strong moral reference points or authorities beyond their own small therapeutic selves and the pain, and often depression, those self-absorbed entities seemed endlessly to recycle. Their rather frenetic activity seemed paradoxically to generate loneliness. And

---

[11]Ibid., 156.

[12]Rohr, "Why Does Psychology Always Win?" *Sojourners* 20 (November 1991): 11.

[13]Richard Sennett, *The Fall of Public Man* (New York: Alfred Knopf, 1977), 3, as cited in Thomas McCollough, *The Moral Imagination and Public Life: Raising the Political Questions* (Chatham, N.J.: Chatham House Publishers, 1991), 63.

[14]Rohr, "Why Does Psychology Always Win?" 11.

with the kind of works righteousness that comes when what you are is signified by what you have and how you wear it, they found no grace.

While self-absorption, distraction, and a periodic wave of real world-weariness may well be factors in explaining the paucity of moral discourse and commitments,[15] the reason goes much deeper and will take longer to address. As Wuthnow found, moral commitment and the formation of character, conscience, and conviction are rooted in the concrete community connectedness of our lives, and that is less and less our experience as adults and as citizens. Furthermore even when some community connectedness is our experience—and community does have tenacity, because people demand it—this connectedness is almost wholly lost to our ways of thinking about moral issues in particular. Deliberating those issues typically uses the noncommunitarian discourse of individual rights and utility or substitutes the language of subjectivity and expressionism for the language of moral obligation. And, as we have seen, responsibility for public life is largely handed over to a market we don't think of or assess in moral terms or a state we don't regard as truly an extension of ourselves. Religious communities are no help, either, if and whenever they serve as a marketplace of largely privatized spiritualities. Liberal moral traditions, which themselves focus on autonomy and rules and procedures, provide only the thinnest base.

Whatever tally we take, the moral emergency we face is that the communities that have given lasting shape to the moral life and perduring substance to moral convictions, from intact families to intact schools and neighborhoods to intact towns and cities with intact ways of life that endure over time and have common memories and practices that anchor shared socialization, are largely gone. The acids of modernity have dissolved these, and the scattered postmodern soul has not restored them. Communities as well as their soils have been depleted. The incapacity to sustain public moral discourse is only one of the victims, and a lesser one

---

[15]In *Learned Optimism* (New York: Random House, 1990). Martin Seligman says that on the basis of his experience as a psychologist working with Alcoholics Anonymous and other twelve-step and self-help groups, he regularly prescribes that members find ways to help other people in order to help them out of "the depression" that comes from overcommitment to the self and "undercommitment to the common good." He says "suffering people" have to "get out of themselves" to break the depression and pain associated with overcommitment to self. He goes on to say that, unfortunately, convincing people of the reasonableness of commitment to the common good is very difficult for the present generation.

at that. Far worse is the concrete human and environmental suffering that society-without-community exacts. Society-without-community is not only a sickness unto death for the moral life; eventually it is deadly for body and soul as well.

So what do we do? It seems misguided, not to say unrealistic, to entertain the nostalgia for small-town America or others of the communities just listed. A cartoon in the *Christian Century* does offer one kind of return. A smiling viewer is listening attentively as the TV announces: "It's the Small-Town Life Soap Opera Network, giving you the security of community ties without the risk of personal human contact."[16]

Another kind of return, more serious, is intimated in the resonance that the appeal to "traditional values," "Judeo-Christian values," or "family values" continues to find. As we noted, politicians who wouldn't dream of honoring them in their own lives still get elected by invoking them. Lasch himself, watching the frazzling of communitarian threads, invites the embrace of a populism that still has some feel for these values. There is something to that. But nostalgia for small-town America and traditional values can mean other things, equally misguided, as Lasch also notes but does not sufficiently absorb into his championing of populism. The very last thing this nation needs, as multicultural, multiracial, and multireligious as it factually is (though is not in its dominant consciousness, habits, or story), is to return the moral life to the homogeneity of like-minded little communities who value that social harmony which comes by shunning, even excluding, the neighbors we don't want as our neighbors. The last thing we need is a society of communities that consider difference to be deviance, which they try to stomp out. Such a society will muster "community" and it will yield clear moral character, firm moral commitments, and strong moral convictions, but it is the morality of bigotry and softer and harder forms of apartheid along lines of race, ethnic group, sexual preference, and class.

Regrettably, housing patterns, educational patterns ("higher" education especially), the suburbanization of America, and the other choices permitted by economic privilege, mean that we already have the modern equivalent of these traditionally constricting and largely homogenous communities—the life-style enclaves we discussed earlier, those look-alike communities with their own brand of irony, that compulsive effort of conforming people to be different and distinctive. In short, while it is

[16]*Christian Century* 108, 29 (1991): 949.

certainly the case that moral communities for a viable civil society will need to draw on myriad traditions, and that there are treasures to be found in pasts both known and forgotten ("the resurgence of buried realities, the reappearance of what was forgotten and repressed," to remember Paz), any repristination of a U.S. past is simply not good enough. The state of modernity-postmodernity means that somehow we fashion moral community from both real commonalities and real differences.

To ask for preindustrial society is even more bizarre, though many conscientious citizens, feeling the spiritual disrepair, are in serious quest of the Arcadian idyll. Often from affluent ranks, they seek membership in circles of intimacy that have nothing to do with the workplace, the neighborhood, or even their own biological families. This is community as pristine retreat for the lucky, and it is often literally in the woods. Its chief virtue seems to be simply that it is away from it all, where "it" is the endless cacophony of the throbbing, phobic world. God knows such retreat is necessary. God also knows it is too part-time, too ad hoc, and too unavailable to be a true base community of moral formation and conviction for most people. "The celebration of rustic felicity was never intended for rustics,"[17] says Lasch, and can only "be savored by people of refinement who did not seriously propose, after all, to exchange the advantages of breeding and worldly experience for a life close to nature, no matter how lyrically they sang nature's praises."[18] In the woods or not, community as retreat will not do. Moral formation takes time and must be forged with regular discipline from the common ingredients and influences in the locales where people live, move, and have their daily being.

The tack of *Habits of the Heart* was to retain the language of community and draw from those historical communities of memory in this society, the churches among them, that have a sense of communal identity and public well-being, communities Bellah et al call the keepers of "biblical and republican" cultural traditions. More precisely, the authors now, in *The Good Society*, want to evoke the lingering communitarianism we still possess as the legacy of such institutions and use it to revitalize the institutions of this society. These institutions, which are in any case

---

[17]Christopher Lasch, *The True and Only Heaven: Progress and Its Critics* (New York: W. W. Norton, 1991), 84.
[18]Ibid.

moral creatures by nature and thus do moral formation, as all patterned human interaction does, would then shape the moral convictions and commitments of the citizenry.

Our approach is a little different, if for no other reason than that the subject is the church in particular, not U.S. society at large. It is noteworthy, nonetheless, that Bellah and company give a large and sympathetic space to "the public church" just as we have given considerable space to U.S. society. In fact the flow of *The Good Society*'s analysis is to the central chapters on "Education: Technical and Moral" and "The Public Church" precisely because these are the institutions that have the most explicit moral vocation in society. With a view to the details of moral vocation, we turn to the nature of the kind of communities modern-postmodern society requires for its own health. We take up the constructive task.

CHAPTER 7

The Ecology of Moral Community

I WRITE THIS ON THE OBSERVANCE OF MARTIN LUTHER KING, JR.'S birthday. His question, "Where do we go from here, chaos or community?" became the title of a book published the year he was assassinated. One of the essays, "The World House," includes this:

> Some years ago a famous novelist died. Among his papers was found a list of suggested plots for future stories, the most prominently underscored being this one: "A widely separated family inherits a house in which they have to live together." This is the great new problem of mankind. We have inherited a large house, a great "world house" in which we have to live together—black and white, Easterner and Westerner, Gentile and Jew, Catholic and Protestant, Moslem and Hindu—a family unduly separated in ideas, culture and interest, who, because we can never again live apart, must learn somehow to live with each other in peace.[1]

King, always "ecological" in his thinking, could be describing not only the planet as a whole but this society in particular. There will soon be more Muslims than Jews in the United States, for example. And in many states, among them the largest and most populated, the next half century will see "a majority of minorities"—no single ethnic group will

[1]Martin Luther King, Jr., *Where Do We Go from Here: Chaos or Community?* (Boston: Beacon Press, 1968), 167.

compose the majority. The world house is here. The big picture plays at the local theater.

Where do we go from here, chaos or community? In part the answer depends on the character of community itself. More precisely it depends on the characteristics of those communities that have moral formation as their explicit moral vocation. And it depends upon whether such communities comprise a critical mass for the kind of civil society the times require.

The Character of Community

"SOCIETY IS NATURALLY COMPOSED NOT OF DISPARATE INDIVIDUALS," Martin Buber wrote, "but of associative units and associations between them."[2] "An organic commonwealth," he went on, "will never build itself up out of individuals but only out of small and ever smaller communities: a nation is a community to the degree that it is a community of communities."[3] Herman Daly and John Cobb's *For the Common Good* elaborates the notion of a society and nation as "a community of communities" and makes the important point that for a society to have a communal character does not require intimacy as such. What it does require is that participation "contributes to self-identification"; that members participate extensively in the decisions by which they are governed; that society as a whole takes responsibility for its members; and that this responsibility includes respect for the diverse individuality of members.[4] Their later discussion adds to this list and emphasizes the character of communitarian relationships as mutual. This means that all members and groups share in both the benefits and the burdens of society, without the benefits falling consistently to some and the burdens to others. It also means that the sacrifices members make are not the kind of sacrifices known in a zero-sum game, that is, more for one party necessarily means less for another. Rather in mutual relations "each loses in the other's

---

[2]Martin Buber as cited by Gar Alperowitz, "Building a Saving Democracy," *Sojourners* 19 (July 1990): 15.
[3]Ibid.
[4]Herman E. Daly and John B. Cobb, Jr., *For the Common Good* (Boston: Beacon Press, 1989), 172.

losses and [each] gains in the other's gains."[5] Sacrifice, then, is not utter loss but that service which sustains and enriches the community that sustains and enriches oneself.

While congeries of relationships that share these characteristics are properly "communities," and while these communities are suggestive precisely because they combine what civil society now most needs (a mix of communitarian and associational ties in viable communities of human scale), more must be said if we are to understand what generates healthy moral formation in particular. Unlike most of the literature offering proposals for curing societal disorder, we cannot simply assume a world of morally formed and responsible citizens. Adequate moral formation itself and the kind of communities it requires are, we have argued at length, what is now most problematic about society. Unfortunately those who do know most about moral development burden us with a parallel omission—they say little about the character of the social arrangements necessary for adequate moral formation, especially political-economic ones, and they fail to detail the kinds of social participation that yields moral well-being in mass society. They describe the "micro" worlds of moral development largely in isolation from the social powers that shape them. They assume "society" just when society as a moral entity is most dubious. We are left, then, with innumerable proposals for society that, like Daly and Cobb, take the requisite basic moral formation utterly for granted; and studies of moral development that, like Kohlberg, Fowler, and Gilligan, say too little about the necessary "macro" social structures and the nature of morally healthy social participation.

Entering this empty intersection in full-dress uniform and ready to direct traffic is the subject of a book, not a chapter. What can be done, however, is a sketch, a sketch of the elements and dynamics of moral community. That will stipulate the kind of communities needed for viable civil society and set the stage for the positive roles of the church as a community of formation and conviction (the next chapter).

Fortunately much of the relevant material has been gathered in one place and helpfully sorted and synthesized, in Philip Selznick's *Moral Commonwealth: Social Theory and the Promise of Community*. As the title indicates, Selznick discusses "The Moral Community" (the last section of the book). Before addressing this, he discusses "Modernity and Morality," "The Moral Person," and "The Moral Institution." We set these

---

[5]Ibid., 188.

aside in favor of the concluding section, where they all converge. Selznick turns to the moral community because the foregoing have all "presumed or invoked a concept of community."[6] We join him there.

His own definition of community as one form of group experience underlines shared beliefs, interests, and commitments around a set of varied activities.[7] Community bonds "establish a common faith or fate, a personal identity, a sense of belonging, and a supportive structure of activities and relationships."[8] Participation touches multiple interests and occurs in various ways. But it doesn't mean that community by definition presumes "locality." Given our earlier discussion of community in chapter 3, and its note that modernity's strong tendency is to make community less a matter of place and more a matter of experience, dropping locality from the requirements is not insignificant. Most important to community, Selznick says, is simply "concerted activity and shared belief."[9] Nonetheless, common residence, while not indispensible, is perhaps the single most "congenial condition"[10] for creating and sustaining community life. It facilitates recurring face-to-face relationships, and these in turn facilitate what the emergence of community most depends on: "the opportunity for, and the impulse toward, comprehensive interaction, commitment, and responsibility."[11]

What most marks community is a way of life that shapes and defines members' identity. Recognizing community does not yet specify or detail its most important elements, however. What are the elements of community, especially those communities essential to moral well-being? Selznick's normative theory of moral community turns on certain variables. We will take each in turn: historicity, identity, mutuality, plurality, autonomy, participation, and integration.[12]

Historicity. Shared history and culture fashion the strongest community bonds. Very general interests and abstract ideas, including moral ideas, make for weak community. The particularities of custom, language, institutional life, demography, and geography, as well as a heri-

[6]Philip Selznick, *The Moral Commonwealth: Social Theory and the Promise of Community* (Berkeley: University of California Press, 1992), 357.
[7]Ibid., 358.
[8]Ibid., 358–59.
[9]Ibid., 359.
[10]Ibid.
[11]Ibid.
[12]Ibid., 361ff.

tage of significant events and crises—these give a community its character, its moral character included.[13]

We noted at the conclusion of chapter 4 that the Enlightenment sought a nonparticular, rational basis for social cooperation. It sought to transcend conflicting particularities with a world ethic composed of moral rules applicable to all and grounded in shared human reason. That we all belong to "the community of reason" was sufficient membership, Enlightenment philosophers argued; shared history was not required. Selznick, though indebted to Enlightenment liberalism, rejects this contention. Peoples' particularities generate and sustain moral community. Morality that does not account for them, draw from them, and channel their passions will fail, as will community. We are particular beings rooted in time and place who find our moral identity through a "narrative" understanding of our lives. We express in our very being the history and the communities of which we are a part.[14] Without them we are morally nowhere.

Historicity, then, has prima facie moral worth, a presumption of favorable moral standing. In Selznick's words, "rootedness and belonging make for individual well-being as well as commitment to others, and a sense of history is needed for collective judgment."[15] Moral wisdom emerges from special experience and a distinct ethos, just as moral principles, though often treated in the form of abstract moral teaching, are latent in a community's culture and have whatever power they have by virtue of their ability to offer concrete guidance. Moral communities, like individuals, will do better and be better, then, if they understand their possibilities and limits. These are best ascertained by knowing where a community has been, presently is, and seems to be going.

For all these reasons, Selznick grants historicity prima facie moral worth as an element of moral community. But it is not more than that,

---

[13]Ibid.

[14]In Christian ethics the work of Stanley Hauerwas, drawing on Alasdair MacIntyre, has been especially important on this subject. Among his many writings, *A Community of Character: Toward a Constructive Christian Social Ethic* (Notre Dame: University of Notre Dame Press, 1981), is of special importance in this regard. My gratitude goes to Elizabeth Bounds and her doctoral dissertation work for the fuller discussion of historicity and moral community, supplementary to Selznick. Of course I can incorporate only a small portion of that ongoing work here, and then only indirectly.

[15]Selznick, *Moral Commonwealth*, 361.

since any given history might mean a community's moral deformation, not health. There are histories and cases of "belonging" we need to break from and discard, just as there are cultures and ways of life that suffocate and oppress rather than nourish and free. Much shared history needs nothing so much as a graceful end, together with a fresh start for members, either together or with others. Shared history and culture, then, have prima facie moral standing much as we might say friendship has. It, too, is an element of moral well-being, a mark of sound community, even a necessity of the good life. But some friendships harm one friend or another. They intensify, even generate, pathologies rather than heal them. They lead to ill-chosen paths rather than socially responsible bonds and endeavors. Thus Selznick argues that historicity, like friendship, is important enough to be presumptive for moral community. But it is not all, and shared history and belonging is as subject to moral criticism as anything else in the moral life.

Identity. Formed identity is the outcome of socialization, and socialization is largely carried out in and through various communities—including families, schools, and religious communities. Indeed identity formation is largely what moral communities are about. Every effort to create moral community will thus draw on the elements of identity and fashion it through socialization processes. This is basic social and moral process.

Yet Selznick says that "of all the elements of community, the moral worth of a formed identity is the most problematic."[16] The many identities formed in various communities—religious, ethnic, economic, familial—are the sources of "virulent antagonisms," which, when crowding the wider public scene, can destroy common community.[17] A strong sense of "we" seems to generate a correspondingly strong sense of "them." Thus the security and even self-esteem rooted in close community may at the same time be purchased at the cost of more inclusive and integrated communities and societies. This does not diminish the importance of identity to community and community to identity. But it does push to the fore the moral question of what kinds of persons are being formed by what kinds of communities. It also raises the question of whether the "we" essential to moral community can be an inclusive one, or whether hostile moral tribalism is our ineluctable fate. Since modernity-postmodernity is by definition a world of interdepen-

[16]Ibid., 362.
[17]Ibid.

dent strangers on a crowded planet, the problem of community and identity, and its resolution, is as vital to everyone's concern as any of the attributes of community and life together. Can pluralism and "otherness" be a mark of close community itself?

Mutuality. Moral community begins with and is largely supported by "the experience of interdependence and reciprocity."[18] Community will neither emerge nor last if people do not need one another or if nothing is to be gained by cooperation. Yet simple exchange or coordinated action for specific goals is not of itself mutuality, any more than association is community. The kind of mutuality that characterizes moral community is open-ended, rather than limited or "contractual," obligation, and it takes place within relationships of trust and caring. Morever, Selznick says, persons are "implicated" as "unities,"[19] and not involved in only partial or segmented ways. That is, they are not primarily occupiers of specified roles with fixed functions but are present as the persons they are in a web of "unfinished," ongoing relationships. Good community "implicates" people in this way, and it means that moral community is always more than simple exchange and voluntary interaction. The movement of moral community is in fact from initial exchange into more enduring bonds of interdependence and commitment. It is a movement from often casual beginnings in "bare-bones mutuality"[20] to continuing relationships and high stakes, a movement from reciprocity and "fellowship" into communion.

Not all healthy moral communities engage members this profoundly and intensely all the time, nor do they need to. But, Selznick argues, they do require the interdependence and reciprocity—mutuality—that lies down this path. By contrast, the part-time, part-person, "contracted" obligations of most of modernity's relationships are not and cannot be the substance of community.

Plurality. Selznick's discussion of plurality as a normative element of community echoes our earlier discussion of society on the model of market and state. Like many other social theorists, Selznick concludes that significant membership in a variety of groups of reasonable human scale—familial, occupational, recreational, ethnic, and religious, for example—extends and enriches community and prevents the loss of community and moral base that happens when very little stands between

[18]Ibid.
[19]Ibid.
[20]Ibid.

individual persons, on the one hand, and impersonal authorities and forces, on the other. A "totalizing" of life at the hands of necessary but impersonal structures of mass governance or at the hands of necessary but impersonal economic forces may secure some essential social outcomes, as we noted earlier. But this totalizing is a dead end as a substitute for moral community. Moral well-being is not guaranteed by the sheer existence of plural "intermediate" communities, of course. Yet intermediate communities, too, have prima facie moral worth, not least because membership in such communities contributes to the social order in ways that extend people's concrete moral responsibility and match their varied interests. The vitality of civil society is largely at stake in the presence and well-being of such communities.

Autonomy. Pluralist groups, however, can be as oppressive as the state and as brutal as the not-so-free market. Community identity, authority, and even integrity can run roughshod over individual members. Their flourishing as responsible persons and effective moral agents may be curtailed rather than developed by their communities. For this reason, personal autonomy is a further mark of normative moral community. Against common distortions of personal autonomy, we must say that it does not mean "unconditional opportunity and choice"[21]—the very slogan of 1980s-style liberation—nor does it posit the unencumbered individual as the basic moral unit of society. Rather, personal autonomy means that within the complex of relationships of which I am part, or might be, self-directed moral agency is cherished and the community itself is measured by its contribution to the flourishing of unique and responsible persons.[22] Thus freedom in associations as well as freedom of association is a moral good to be protected by community itself, as well as society.[23] Genuine autonomy is the responsible self-direction of the person as a social self and community member.

Participation. Personal autonomy and moral agency can be realized only in and through social participation.[24] But what kind of participation makes and keeps moral community moral? The most rudimentary and essential activities are also the most important and have to do with life's basic continuities—child rearing, work, kinship and friendship relations,

---

[21]Ibid., 363.
[22]Ibid.
[23]Ibid.
[24]Ibid.

rules and customs for life together, festivity. Broader contexts and enterprises build on these and are weakened when these are weak.

These basic communal activities all engage the kind of participation Selznick names "core," as contrasted with "segmental," participation.[25] An extended look at each—core and segmental—is necessary. Ultimately at stake is the peculiar and indispensable place of "base moral communities" for societies in the modern-postmodern world.

No one doubts that social participation and human character are decisively affected by social ethos and structures and the patterning and channeling of behavior they effect.[26] If we imagine the same child raised in very different societies, or imagine a young, zealous German doctor emigrating to New Zealand in 1943 just before he was to join the corps "servicing" the concentration camps, we can begin to understand how ethos and structures shape human conduct and character. Strengths and weaknesses we often attribute abstractly to human nature are decisively affected by patterned ways of relating and belonging. Among other things they affect what Selznick calls "moral recalcitrance, regression and frailty,"[27]—what Christians have included in discussions of "sin." That is, morally undesirable actions are furthered or restrained by different cultural and social patterns. The nature and quality of our moral experience is affected by the nature and quality of our participation in the arrangements we sum up as "society."[28]

Having established the nature of social participation as critical to moral community and well-being, Selznick discusses at some length two ways of participating in society and its moral order—the aforementioned ways of "core" and "segmental" participation. His purpose is not only to describe why the former is critical to moral community but also to answer a quite specific moral question: "What does it require to be genuinely other-regarding and, at the same time, genuinely self-preserving?" The answer moves along the following lines.

Core participation belongs in the first place to the primary groups and intimate associations that do the chief work of socialization and from which we draw throughout life. Families are the universal, but not only,

---

[25]Ibid., 184.

[26]For one account of this, see the chapter "Character and Social Structure," in Bruce C. Birch and Larry L. Rasmussen, *Bible and Ethics in the Christian Life*, 2d ed. (Minneapolis: Augsburg, 1989), 85–99.

[27]See Selznick's discussion, *Moral Commonwealth*, 171–182.

[28]Ibid., 183.

example. If we possess psychological strength and moral competence, Selznick argues, it is likely an expression of healthy primary relations.

But this raises the question about the salient features of primary relations, and thus of core participation. Selznick's list includes, first, whole person, rather than segmental, response.[29] Our response to others in settings of core participation takes account of many aspects of personality, background, and behavior. It is an unguarded and largely spontaneous response that lets feelings color communication and judgment.[30] Such participation is most fully expressed as love and friendship.

Primary relations also deal with intrinsic worth. What counts is who people are, where they belong, and what their unique particularity is, rather than their particular accomplishments and proven capacities or their "fit" for a certain social slot or role. As Selznick puts it, their value is "ascriptive," and they need not be on guard or appeal to "rights" in order to enter the human exchange or relationship.[31]

Community interaction as core participation also involves open communication and trust, "being open to influence, and influence in depth."[32] It means a relatively free flow of thoughts and emotions.

Another characteristic is mutual, open-ended obligation. A spirit of bracketed, carefully circumscribed obligation is alien to primary relations and core social participation. The terms of some prospective agreement are less the center of attention than the participating persons and their relationship.[33] Here Selznick adds, with insight, that every intimate association does not a primary relationship make. "Encounter groups," for example, are "a poor substitute for genuine primary relations."[34]

Common identity and belonging, a sense of "we," also characterizes the members of primary groups. But this does not mean their participation in one another's lives is always cordial. The web of relationships may well be "a cauldron within which resentments simmer and hostilities erupt."[35] Yet "we-ness" has a grip, and even amid the fights a positive valuation of the group may very well hold firm, together with a concomitant sense of investment. Often it is only at the point of exiting such a

[29]Ibid., 190.
[30]Ibid.
[31]Ibid., 190–91.
[32]Ibid., 191.
[33]Ibid.
[34]Ibid.
[35]Ibid.

group that the level of investment is fully discovered. This only underscores how "core" the participation has been.

In addition, personal development, security, and satisfaction are uppermost in primary relations, according to Selznick. Core participation thus influences people deeply at whatever age and in whatever circumstances. Development, security, and satisfaction are not age-, time-, or place-specific.

Core participation is central to moral competence, then, because it is central in the socialization that makes us the kinds of persons we are. It is the sort of participation that, more than any other, shapes moral character and forms conscience. It disposes us to be governed by the moral concerns we have learned and internalized as second nature. It engenders certain moral sensibilities and transmits certain moral beliefs. Moral mentoring happens in these primary relations through core participation. Getting along as newborn moral animals is passed along here in this way.

The success of moral socialization is, of course, highly varied. Moral quality can range from splendid to depraved, not least because of the effect on primary groups of broader social patterning and channeling of behavior. As a consequence, moral assessment of primary group health and core participation, as well as social structures, is a part of any serious ethic. But the place of core participation in moral competence (or lack thereof) is not thereby changed. Core participation is crucial, for better and for worse.

We add that primary relations and core participation do not constitute all of morality, and they have their own intrinsic costs. These relations often bear heavy emotional tolls and strain our capacity for extensive, open-ended obligation. They often create a narrow, constricted moral universe and leave us formed as a tight "we" group set within a bewildering world or against a threatening one. Nonetheless, primary relations and core participation have prima facie moral worth because moral competence cannot happen apart from basic socialization at the hands of a "parent" generation. That of itself, to underscore an important point yet again, does not guarantee that socialization will be of high moral quality, or even minimally sufficient. But it does guarantee its necessity.

Selznick's second form of social participation—segmental—is as necessary to the moral life in modern-postmodern society as core participation. It facilitates cooperation with modernity's mass of interdependent strangers. Its archetype is perhaps, as Selznick claims, the commercial contract, which presumes and spells out limited, but real, obligation.[36] But it functions as well in the specifications of law and governance that channel our responsibilities as tax-paying, vote-casting citizens. Segmental participation is the kind most involved in the moral accomplishments of market and state discussed earlier (chap. 4). Its terms are determinate rather than open-ended, fixed in their responsibilities and demands. In segmental relationships we generally know where we stand and what is expected of us. We can measure our psychic and social investment with some degree of accuracy. We can maintain necessary distance as well as fulfill necessary duties.

All this makes for moral orderliness in a world of countless routine interactions. Segmental participation is that species of social participation which is particularly well tuned to societies with market economies and mass institutions and is without doubt indispensable to them and their accomplishments.

Yet many of the moral qualities of this kind of participation are liabilities for both self and society. The very characteristics that make it work—participation that is limited, instrumental, peripheral to our most important relationships and concerns—are qualities that undermine strong moral fabric. In societies driven by urbanization, industrialization, and technological development, segmental participation easily becomes the dominant mode, to the undoing of more person-centered, caring, spontaneous, communitarian relationships.[37] Segmental participation is effective as an instrument that harnesses human energies for mass ends. It specializes, mobilizes, and coordinates well. But in the very process it yields people who from a psychological and moral point of view are largely uncommitted. Their sense of personal responsibility is weakened by "partial participation" (Selznick's synonym for segmental) and their (learned) psychic distance often leaves them bereft of deep feeling and attachment. This in turn means they are susceptible to fad, fantasy, and illusion, and to managed communication and "collective excitement."[38] Differently said, weak personal commitment means vulnerability to emotional manipulation, gamesmanship, and exploitation.

More than this, a society characterized primarily by segmental participation experiences a subtle and paradoxical relationship between

[36]Ibid., 184.
[37]Ibid., 188.
[38]Ibid., 189.

selective, bracketed commitment and "total" mobilization and involvement. Persons driven at any given moment by a single passion—anger, lust, envy, greed—may be drawn into a total, though destructive, commitment and activity. They may quite easily become wholly absorbed and find any number of channels for their obsession. In the psychology of collective behavior, including the social movements of civil society, "total" and "segmental" participation may well be reflexes of each other.[39]

In short, lacking healthy communities of core participation, many people "totalize" segmental activity, becoming in effect "consumers" of inauthentic, though intense, substitutes for community. The alternative, then, is not segmental participation or total involvement; as indicated, they easily combine for compulsive, impulse-driven behavior. The alternative is core participation in intimate communities with the qualities mentioned above. The alternative is communitarian relationships in primary groups that supplement and enrich necessary associational ones. Core participation and its ethos is itself a mark of normative moral community and healthy society.

Integration. Selznick mentions this element last for a reason. It is certainly a quality of moral community. But it is the one that properly balances or mixes the others. Historicity and the givenness of received ways is important for community but must be balanced against the dynamics of plurality and be open to where they might lead. The claims of plurality and autonomy need to take account of those of mutuality and participation and not sacrifice communal bonds on the altar of a notion of unbounded "freedom." Identity has its own requirements and claims, but they cannot be absolutized either. Integration, then, is that moral quality of community which displays the community's capacity to maintain its chief values by keeping them in working tension and balance and encouraging their development and interchange.[40]

There is no recipe for this. Communities are living moral entities with differing histories and character; they will thus show different mixes of the same or similar elements. Perhaps most important is the communities' need simply to be aware of their critical moral qualities and subject them to collective assessment (this is part of the task of moral critique discussed in chapter 1).

---

[39]Ibid.
[40]Ibid., 364.

With Selznick's important contribution on the marks of moral community in hand, we go on to related discussions of the ecology of such community. Two topics come to mind. The first is the need for communities of intimacy in a world hard on intimacy. What morally is at stake in such communities, especially when considered with a view to the meaning of childhood for the moral life? The second is the contextualizing of moral community in our kind of society. In view of the dynamics of modernity-postmodernity, what are its specific moral tasks and the "internal" requirements for its own effective presence?

While Daly and Cobb, mentioned before, are right that the communities that build up a society, à la Buber, need not all be characterized by intimacy, some of them must be. Why? Selznick's discussion of core participation and primary group relations is an important start. But more must be said. More must be said about the particular place of childhood and youth in the moral life, about our early character-forming and conscience-forming years. Since we are chasing the basics of moral community and assuming nothing, what is obvious to many readers must nonetheless be stated simply for reasons of its importance, and no other.

From the point of view of moral analysis, modern institutions tend to forget the same thing the Enlightenment did, that we are children before we are adults. This is to say that our formation as moral beings begins well before we ourselves make any significant moral choices and even before we show evidence of moral consciousness at all, much less considered moral reflection. The examined life, the only kind Socrates thought worth living, is down a long trail into the future from the onset of the moral life itself. Much that is considered the proper conduct of life itself, once examination does come to morally conscious youth and adults, is set down near the beginnings of the life venture, back in those prehistoric days when we were toddlers and preschool terrorists. Granted, we have few conscious memories of that essential formation. But deep subconscious memories, written on the heart and inscribed in the nascent soul, stay with us in daily ways. Moral identity itself begins when the first contours of personality and temperament are set down, well before we said our first complete sentence or learned which part of the book was the "front." It begins when the texture of life is present to us in the form of our very first companions, when dispositions toward life are sculpted in their most elementary and important ways. (Whether life is trustworthy or not is largely determined in the parent-infant bond, to cite one example.) Learning is principally imitation (including moral imitation). The rudiments of right and wrong, acceptable and unacceptable behavior, are inculcated as the first spoken and unspoken catechisms. And the basic social graces (too tepid a term for learning how to treat one another) are first acquired in a hundred small ways spread across any given week.

This list of elements could be extended but need not. They all arrive at the same double conclusion: Our most basic moral learning is prior to the "reason" with which we might eventually question, clarify, and extend it, and the communities of intimate others first work this crucial moral work. This is where the world itself is first transmitted and the ways of culture originally learned. This is where character is fashioned. ("Character" is from the Greek *charakter*, meaning "engraving tool" and, by extension, the marks made by the engraving tool.) Here, when people are most tender, is where and when moral formation, including malformation, most happens. If self-worth and self-affirmation are to happen, for example, their seeds should be planted in these tender years. "God lays souls into the lap of married people" is Luther's comment,[41] to which we add of the unmarried, too.

Understanding the moral personhood of children, then, is not best gained by interrogating their own limited moral vocabulary and its utterances, nor by studying them as individuals. "Discourse" and the child as some separate individual mean little. These budding moral persons are best understood by looking to the moral quality of their limited communities and the practices and conditions of these communities in the midst of the larger society bearing down on them. They are best understood by looking to the quality of the core participation in the child's primary world. Later the children's worlds will expand. New relationships will multiply quickly and older ones evolve significantly. The moral life will then take on other hues as children learn to enter and live in new circles. Later, too, making significant moral choices will happen by gradation and in keeping with circumstances over which the children have varying degrees of control. The point remains that none of us traffics in universal behaviors expressive of universal reason or irrepressible natural law; we traffic in the unavoidably particular cultures of communities present to us in concrete ways in specific places. And the first of these, both chronologically and by virtue of life significance, are communities of intimacy and core participation.

---

[41]From Herbert Brokering and Roland Bainton, *Luther's Germany* (Minneapolis: Augsburg, 1985), 45.

These communities may be atrocious, carefree, stifling, violent, warm and convivial, protective, pedestrian, almost magical, or some combination. The occasion of moral formation is also the occasion of malformation. Current statistics on intimate violence, malnutrition, abuse, and neglect are chilling evidence of close community gone terribly wrong or rendered unworkable by societal forces. The level of women and children in poverty in this society paints the same picture.[42] Yet the point is that for better and for worse we are first formed in these communities of time and place. So we are loving, fierce, hateful, open, caring, or withdrawn at home or in school, on the street or in a bar, at church or at work, in Kalamazoo, Peoria, or some farm in Georgia. We take up a culture, a way of life, that we make our own in networks of intimacy that were making us the kinds of persons we are long before we ever knew.[43] Only a serious case of amnesia forgets how critical these communities are to society, just as only a case of grave social irresponsibility neglects their well-being. They ground the moral life, they ground society's life. What is public is first personal.

Differently said, we are essentially and not accidentally community moral beings. The self is fundamentally communal. That being the case, the issue becomes the kind and quality of the communities constituting civil society. We have argued only that communities of intimacy—networks of emotional bonds and mutuality in a closely shared existence—are among the most important members in the constellation of society's communities of moral formation and that these are communities of a certain kind with a necessarily limited scale. This is the meaning of the African proverb that it takes a village to raise a child. That noted, we go on to further characterize requisite moral communities in this society.

---

[42]See the report *Women and Children Living in Poverty: A Report to the Evangelical Lutheran Church in America with Recommendations for Action*, December 1989, revised February 1991 (Columbus, Ohio: The Institute for Mission in the U.S.A., Trinity Lutheran Seminary).

[43]This discussion is a trimmed-down version of a more detailed argument by Shannon M. Jordan in "The Moral Community and Persons," *Philosophy Today*, Summer 1986, 108–17. She argues, correctly in my judgment, that "*culture, or moral community, is* the empirical condition of being human" (115, her emphasis). Differently said, the person is constituted by the relations of persons, and these are present to us in and as communities. We are essentially, not accidentally, communal beings.

Communities Needed

EARLIER CHAPTERS TRACED THE CORROSIVE EFFECTS OF MODERNITY ON the communities of civil society. This includes the base moral communities of intimacy just mentioned. What we have not discussed in sufficient detail, despite Selznick's contribution, is the nature of the communities now required to negotiate a convulsive world. Can we say more about the kind of communities needed to do the moral formation not effectively attended to by market and by state; that is, the kind of communities needed to fashion morality inspired "neither by a rational quest after self-interest nor by a fear of coercive external authority"?[44] This is, after all, the morality that allows the institutions of economy and government to work in the first place. They work only because people by and large trust one another, that is, they take one another at their word and keep it. They work because people do not take bribes as standard business practice or serve only their friends. They work because not all citizens press their rights and legitimate demands simultaneously but are willing to engage in give-and-take on the assumption that reciprocity and fair play will and do exist. They work because the law is accepted as a legitimate authority. They work because people by and large obey traffic signals, pay their taxes, and serve on juries. They work because people consider themselves responsible for their own actions. The great social systems work only because a modicum of nonmarket and noncoerced morality functions reasonably well.

Of itself this is not enough, however. The conditions of society amid forced experimentation and realignments of all kinds, indeed of morality itself in the making around new issues and old, all press further requirements. These requirements mean that a certain kind of community is needed for the morality civil society itself needs. Its profile moves along the following lines, supplementing and concretizing Selznick's discussion of moral community.

Against modern technology's reduction of moral agency and imagination to compartmentalized labor and distracting consumption as a way of life, and against its loss of nature, culture, and social relations as common reference points of meaning and commitment, communities of healthy civil society work to exhibit core participation that is simulta-

---

[44]Alan Wolfe, *Whose Keeper? Social Science and Moral Obligation* (Berkeley, Los Angeles, London: University of California Press, 1989), 188.

neously "manifold engagement." These communities are places of multilayered interaction among human beings (and nonhuman ones), where traditions and rituals are developed and preserved, skills are learned and utilized, discipline is expected and nurtured, and fidelity and accountability to community members is practiced.

Against both the workings of technology and the ways of the market, which care not at all for community, memory, or history, communities of civil society are places of memory and hope. Memory in these open enclaves includes the span of the generations who make up the communities but reaches as well into the formative narratives and lifeways of ages past and places remote. Retelling the stories of beginnings and of survival is especially important, not least because it fuels present hope. This hope not only energizes the present generation, however; it extends its circle of care to generations yet unborn and to their requirements for life. In brief, these are communities that structure immediate experience into a personalized culture with a conscious historical framework and a clear horizon of expectation. Members are schooled into shared patterns of language, behavior, rites, and symbols that cross expanses of time and space.

Against the (necessary) impersonality of both market and state as moral proxies, and against the slow, steady transformation of community by modernity into enclaves of conforming privacy, communities of able civil society "major" in the personal as public and the public as diverse. They foster membership that, in a contracting world, cuts across society's clusters of varied citizens and enjoys the mix in ways that contribute both to the life of individual communities and the wider public. Their morality is that of smaller "publics" contributing their part as specialized, complex cells of the body politic.

Against the second bourgeois revolution's doctrine of the calculating self, these communities cultivate a sense of self that knows that its well-being resides in the well-being of others, and theirs in its. Against the ethos of the 1980s, these communities understand that genuine morality is other-regarding, self-engaging, community oriented, public, and reciprocal.

Before all this escalates to levels that claim far too much and unwittingly substitute renewed community for Bacon's *Novum Organum* or the dollar bill's *novus ordo seclorum*, we must draw distinctions. What more can we say about these communities that shows their fit with a modern-postmodern world and at the same time limits their work to the plausible and necessary?

Daly and Cobb insisted that the communities of civil society need not be intimate ones, and in that connection we noted that both communitarian and associational ties are desirable and necessary. In a highly mobile world, many of the communities of civil society should have dimensions of belonging and strong group loyalty at the same time they gather and send forth members with some ease. Not everyone need know everyone else, but the sense of personal presence and contribution does need to be felt. These communities should also be able to make alliances and join, movement fashion, in making common cause for the common good. The "ecclesiology," then, is a cell-and-movement ecclesiology, with communitarian and associational dimensions throughout.

The combination of communitarian and associational ties is difficult and, for our kind of world, necessary. This is community that is neither the organism of premodern communities nor the artifact of society as the contract of autonomous individual citizens exercising segmental participation as their prime experience. The mix of communitarian and associational is not new, but it is not well developed, either. Because we have spoken primarily of communitarian dimensions (with more coming in the next chapter), something more should be said about associational ties, again supplementing Selznick's discussion.

The associational ties in view here are not the "I-Thou" bonds of intimacy or the "I-It" relationship of subject to object. They are subject-to-subject in a community of interests, once tagged by Harvey Cox as "I-You" connections. That is, we are genuinely connected, and the purpose of our association together is to contribute both to one another's welfare and the wider society's, but we remain strangers and go our separate ways, only to repeat this same alliance with others in other communities or with one another again in the public space we share. Parents and teachers in the parent-teacher association, members of a neighborhood community board working on a project together, and churches organizing in advocacy for low-income housing are but three among examples too numerous to mention.

Associational ties are the most common ones now. For many people they are the preponderant ones on any given day. Any serious treatment of moral formation must include dynamics and ask how persons who are strangers to one another can fashion healthy moral relationships together. In different words, what are the marks of those moral communities which are not in the first instance characterized by primary relations but by changing membership whose participation is a mix of occasionally communitarian ties but predominately associational ones?

Most helpful to this question would be a discussion of the place of "interests" and "boundaries" as requirements of viable communities now.

In the modern-postmodern world, a "community of interests" of some kind is no doubt needed for community itself. Community by definition involves joining with others, sharing some common purposes, and undertaking some common actions to achieve them. Not all members need hold all purposes in common nor act as a unit on every matter. But there must be an overlapping of members' interests, a "comm-unity" of interests. The community is not simply each individual member's interests writ large; rather, collective interests draw the individual beyond the place she or he started and into a network of open response and responsibility.

"Open" response and responsibility does not mean vague and undirected. Healthy communities draw boundaries and make focal points and practices clear. Community with any staying power is impossible without them. Group identity depends on closure, though not rigidity. Amid the turmoil of modernity, the more elusive the boundaries, the more likely community is not community at all but random association headed for identity confusion and dissipation. Just as people without membership in communities are lost (Walzer argues that membership in communities is the primary good we distribute to one another),[45] so communities without boundaries are lost. It may be especially the case, as Selznick and many others have argued, that communities of character require stable, ongoing associations of persons with special commitments to one another, a common purpose, and a common sense of life; we only underscore that all this assumes and requires reasonably clear community boundaries.[46]

But what do effective boundaries themselves require, at least minimally? "Tolerance" is a chief liberal virtue and a precious one. It is certainly crucial for civil society in the crowded and boisterous world of modernity and postmodernity. We do not begin to exercise it well enough and pay a terrible price. But tolerance is not community and does not, of itself, generate community, though it often saves and preserves it. It is an important brake on oppressive community boundaries; on its own, however, tolerance does not establish boundaries.

A clearer minimum requirement for community definition (and thus boundaries) is loyalty. Loyalty is faithfulness and a studied commitment to take others seriously in season and out. Its corollary, or perhaps

---

[45]Michael Walzer, *Spheres of Justice* (New York: Basic Books, 1983), 31.
[46]Ibid., 62–63.

ground, is a certain kind of respect, a respect more bestowed or granted than earned—the social expression, if you will, of the grace by which God invests more trust in us and takes more chances with us than we have coming. Here dignity is conferred as a matter of membership, then simply assumed as that which is due each member in a relationship of loyalty to one another.[47] Hannah Arendt even claims that this kind of respect is to the larger domain of human affairs what love is in more circumscribed circles. It is, she says, a kind of "friendship" "without intimacy and without closeness"[48] but with a regard for persons independent of particular qualities we may cherish or achievements we may esteem.[49] Arendt goes on to lament "the modern loss of [such unconditioned] respect" and the substitute for it of the conviction that respect is due only where and when we fasten on some quality or accomplishment we admire or esteem. This constitutes "a clear symptom of the increasing depersonalization of public and social life."[50]

Boundaries defined by this respect and loyalty are genuine boundaries. They include but they also exclude. They permit a wide sweep for tolerance, but they do not permit everything. They do not, for example, allow membership fundamentally opposed to the existence of people as a people—the Klan rejection of Jews, Catholics, or blacks, for example, or some wealthy people's principled rejection of the poor. Positively said, community concerns can be rather diffuse, and the characters who make up the community very diverse—many can even be strangers—if members are ready for one another in ways that assume and show this acceptance and loyalty, ways that reflect a largely unguarded welcome of one another rooted in conferred respect. Interests can be highly varied, range widely in scope, evolve in their character, and be held to in different constellations if these kinds of bonds are present, establishing these kinds of wide, but genuine, boundaries. Certainly more than an intellectual interest in one another is needed for such boundaries, but the ardor of per-

---

[47]Readers may wish to consult James M. Gustafson's discussion of the classic theological virtues—faith, hope, and love—as the requisites of even secular community. See his essay "The Moral Conditions Necessary for Human Community," in *Christian Ethics and the Community* (Philadelphia: Pilgrim Press, 1971), 153–63.

[48]Hannah Arendt, *The Human Condition* (Chicago: University of Chicago Press, 1958), 243.

[49]Ibid.

[50]Ibid.

sonal love as an emotion, for example, is not. To be underlined is that the unity of a closed system of doctrine or binding kinship, ethnic, political, or religious ties are not boundary-setting requirements of moral formation here. An urban neighborhood of highly diverse membership can be a rich base moral community, for example, and some are. Nonetheless many communities of moral formation will have close kinship, ethnic, or other ties of unity, as well as deep bonds of personal love. But these are not indispensable stipulations. Loyalty and respect are. When loyalty and respect set the boundaries, people can disagree with one another, even fight with one another, over controversial moral issues. They can entertain considerable pluralism without forsaking community. Indeed, the pluralism is itself a stipulation for rich moral community.

For society's sake, and thus our own, we must underscore moral community as people who are both in one another's bodily and emotional presence with some regularity and who themselves might well be a highly diverse lot with shifting collective interests. Modernity-postmodernity cannot tolerate either the loss of close communities or the presence of communities that destroy difference. We cannot afford either the anonymity and moral homelessless of individualism or the separation and violence of tight communities organized around tribal consensus of one kind or another. (Our examples at the outset were Christian Afrikanerdom and expressions of medieval Christendom. Now in our own society treatment of gay and lesbian persons and racial equality are litmus tests.) The search is for communities of mutual acceptance that at the same time respect and work from difference. They are characterized by common attachment and deep self-involvement, but their identity is not utter identification, nor their unity conformity.

It is vital to recognize that we are speaking about such communities as base communities of moral formation and not about society as a whole. That does not mean society may not share some of these characteristics. It means that close community as a model of society itself is unrealizable in a world where millions of interdependent people will necessarily remain strangers. Close, diverse community is absolutely necessary to the moral health of society but it is impossible as a model for all social relations. We may well argue for the good society as one in which decentralized and interdependent units work out regional economic and political networks and maximize the opportunities for consensus democracy. Too little of this has been tried in an era of giant organizations, especially with a view to geographical regions as self-sustaining "bioregions." In this way, our communities might be significant structural elements of society itself. Still, close community is a pipe dream as a model for society as a whole in a world already borderless across great expanses and in need of stronger global connections as well as local ones. Nor would it work as the chief form for those whose home is one of the "megapolis" urban regions where the majority of human beings now live. Innumerable voluntary communities can certainly exist in mass urban areas, and do. The point is simply that they cannot be the organizing principle for the whole society in such areas, or elsewhere.[51] Large institutions with other means are necessary.[52]

In any case, the attempt to make community everything denies the historical reality in which we live. In its own way, it is as illusory as thinking that market and state can suffice as models of society, or that the rule of law and enough police, courts, and jails can substitute for civil society. Paradoxically the very society that most tries to use the market for society, the United States, also tries hardest to use the voluntary communities of civil society to redress social ills largely created by socioeconomic dynamics. "A thousand points of light" are to solve issues of homelessness, hunger, substandard school performance and dropouts, environmental degradation, domestic violence, deteriorating neighborhoods, fractured families, conflicts of race, and any number of other matters of social welfare. This is asking the communities of civil society to be more than they can possibly be. (Invariably it is also to send these communities chasing after the symptoms and consequences, rather than the causes, of social problems.)

What we are seeking is crucial but infinitely more modest; namely, that kind of gracious domain in which, amid caring for others and they for us, we learn the art of understanding the moral positions of others so

---

[51]This discussion is a friendly exchange with Iris Marion Young, already cited in Linda J. Nicholson, ed., *Feminism/Postmodernism* (New York and London: Routledge, 1990). I wholly concur that intimate communities cannot be a model for society. But I disagree with her that close community always and necessarily means a suffocating, oppressive one. She disavows the notion of community altogether, except for a loophole in the closing paragraph, and does so because she identifies community with tight congeries of relationships that suppress and subsume differences (what we have referred to as traditional or premodern communities). I think she thereby fails to perceive both the need for communities of intimacy in modernity and the possibility that such communities need not replicate the totalistic communities she sees as the only possible kind.

[52]The "moral institution" is a crucial subject in its own right and worthy of book-length treatment. But we cannot take it up here. Readers are directed to the major section on this subject in Selznick's volume, 229–354.

indispensable to public life itself.[53] Most of these communities are voluntary, they affirm individual dignity without enshrining individualism, and they exercise authority. But it is authority that members themselves generate, to which they consent, and for which they themselves are accountable.[54]

It remains to be said that these very communities necessarily enter the tumultuous social experimentation that modernity-postmodernity pushes on us. Their contribution is most substantial when it works consciously at a visible way of life and the practices integral to it. Amid unavoidable experimentation, few things are as helpful as manifest community ways of life that signal possibilities for society on a grander scale. The communities of which we speak can thus be the birthplaces and living laboratories for renewed civil society. Indeed, as argued already, that which is necessary at national and international levels in marketplace and institutions of governance—moral integrity, character, democratic diplomacy, honest deals—is first learned closer to the ground in smaller communities.

To emphasize what was said earlier, if we expect to have viable communities that combine associational and communitarian elements, we must give much more attention to first communities of intimacy, especially the family. Families, neighborhoods, and religious communities are the social creatures most neglected in modernity's considerations of the good life. The virtues, values, obligations, and vision first learned in families (or not learned) is what goes public as our circles expand. The gifts nurtured there (or not nurtured) are the ones played out when people move into the more diffuse webs of association that tie fragile society together. The moral repertoire assembled in intimate circles (or not assembled) is what personalizes actions so that people understand themselves as contributing citizens of society when they act in and through the systems of market and state.

---

[53]Wolfe, *Whose Keeper?* 233.

[54]The discussion here is indebted to John Howard Yoder's chapter "The Hermeneutics of Peoplehood," in his *Priestly Kingdom: Social Ethics as Gospel* (Notre Dame: University of Notre Dame Press, 1984), 22–26. That discussion includes the following sentence: "Voluntary commitment to a community distinct from the total society provides resources for practical moral reasoning of a kind which are by definition unthinkable where that option is not offered and where the only way to be an individual is to rebel" (25).

For Christian ethics, the necessary attention to families and other communities of intimacy must include gender analysis at every step, along with race and class analysis, since women are often saddled with moral nurture and then blamed when it is not done well. For children it is especially important that love and discipline come from the same sources. But these sources should not be restricted to only one or two caretakers. This is too much electricity on too few circuits. In an age of small families, it means that communities and society have to find additional means of showing intimacy to children, or society's own moral formation goes awry. Unfortunately the advent of wage labor and mass production removed men's work from children's experience and psychic development only to be followed by removing women's out-of-home work as well. (Now more than 50 percent of the work force in the U.S. is female.) How the economy can be reordered to take account of changed families and work force, in order to permit proper child rearing, is not clear. But the heavy pressures on families arise largely from economic arrangements and their various costs, including psychosocial ones. In rethinking them, special consideration must therefore be given to justice for women and children. If it is not, society's moral formation will suffer even more not least because the family is "the school of justice" for the larger society, the place children "are first exposed to the models of fairness and unfairness" that later affect their behavior in society.[55]

That the public is first personal is one reason to underscore this connection of intimate communities to the current need for communities that combine associational and communitarian dimensions. The other reason is the nature of uncertain times, of *kairos* as a season, of everything at once. In such times, when inherited patterns and structures creak in the beams and falter, society depends more and more on the moral character of the citizenry to hold things together and keep things reasonably humane. Like Kant, Walter Rauschenbusch argued the power of good social structures to mold behavior and "make bad [people] do good things."[56] But when social structures are themselves problematic and

---

[55]Martha Nussbaum, "Justice for Women!" a review of Susan Moller Okin, *Justice, Gender, and the Family* (New York: Basic Books, 1991) in the *New York Review of Books* 39, 16 (1992): 44.

[56]See Walter Rauschenbusch, *Christianizing the Social Order* (New York: Macmillan, 1912), 127. Readers may wish to consult the discussion of how character is formed, and its relation to social structures, in Birch and Rasmussen, *Bible and Ethics*, chaps. 4 and 5.

dysfunctional, their own evolution and shape depend not only on people with organizational and technical skills but on a sense of responsibility, care, and commitment that resides in character already formed. The tone of society in general in seasons when neighborhoods walk the edges of social breakdown depends upon moral leadership as much as any other. Moreover it is doubtful that diverse moral communities are themselves possible apart from a critical mass of members already reasonably stable in their identity and individuality. Like society at large, these communities draw deeply on character already given shape. All this reinforces the need for attention to the health of families, day care, schools, and other first communities of intimacy. And these again remind us of the scale that base moral communities require. The requisite values—respect, loyalty, tolerance—are themselves short-lived if they are not part of character that has learned trust and experienced mutuality. Mutuality and trust in turn are possible only in communities small enough to permit personal acquaintance and the sense of moral responsibility that issues from direct, face-to-face participation. If small communities do not form this trust and sense of moral responsibility, universal moral appeals—to "rights," for example, or respect for law—have too little backing to be effective. There simply is no substitute for small-scale communities of moral generation. The more "planetary" our lives become, the more necessary small communities are.

Further discussion of communities of moral formation and conviction for our time is the subject of the next chapter. After all, we cannot relate virtues, values, and practices in general to societies in general through communities in general, but only concrete virtues, values, and practices for specific societies at particular times. Lived life resists abstraction with every fiber of its being. The focus of the next chapter is entirely on the churches as such communities, however. Readers should thus keep two things in mind. First, that the characteristics outlined often pertain to more than the churches. There are many communities that might build up civil society via visible ways of life centered in focal practices in the United States at the end of the century. Second, the churches, not being the only brand of such communities, will need to join with others for the renewal of civil society. Making common cause for the common good by way of various alliances is a vital element of the churches' public moral witness. This is part of cell-and-movement ecclesiology. The effort to think in a fresh way about the church as a moral community—the next and last chapter—is not, then, only about the church, even when the focus and detail are.

CHAPTER 8

A People of the Way

IN PAT CONROY'S *PRINCE OF TIDES* THE NARRATOR'S GRANDFATHER, Amos Wingo, is an eccentric barber and seller of Bibles throughout the south who, as a rather frail old gent, struggled alone with a large wooden cross down the main street of Colleton, South Carolina, every Good Friday. It was his sacramental reenactment of the passion of his beloved Lord, Jesus. Only Mr. Fruit, who directed the annually confused traffic, understood. But as comes to all of us, so death also came to Amos Wingo. Tolitha had sent him out for a bottle of A-1 sauce, and, with the bottle just off the shelf and firmly in the grip of his big hand, he gave a small cry and "pitched forward into a canned goods display of turnip greens flavored with pork." "The South died for me that day," grandson Tom tells us,

> or at least I lost the most resonant and eminent part of it. It lost that blithe magic I associate with earned incongruity. [Grandfather] had caught flies and mosquitoes in jars and set them free in the back yard because he could not bear to kill one of God's creatures.
>
> "They're part of the colony," he had said. "They're part of the design."
>
> His death forced me to acknowledge the secret wisdom that issues naturally from the contemplative life. His was a life of detachment from the material and the temporal. As a boy I was embarrassed by the undiluted ardor he brought to worship. As an adult I would envy forever the simplicity and grandeur of his vision of what it was to be a complete and contributing man. His

> whole life was a compliance and a donation to an immaculate faith. When I wept at his funeral, it was not because of my own loss. You carry a man like Amos with you, a memory of an immortal rose in the garden of the human ego. No, I cried because my children would never know him and I knew that I was not articulate enough in any language to describe the perfect solitude and perfect charity of a man who believed and lived every simple word of the book he sold door to door the length and breadth of the American South. The only word for goodness is goodness, and it is not enough.[1]

The subject of this chapter is the church as a "people of the way," the church as a religiously formed way of life. I am keenly aware of the inadequacies that attend describing this people and this way. These earthen vessels are live human beings, who, like Amos Wingo, all have their quirks and drastic shortcomings. "We've got flaws we haven't even used yet," Pogo the theologian reminds us, adding another *bon mot* to his more famous ones: "We have met the enemy and they is us," and "What we face, friends, are insurmountable opportunities." One can finally only tell of them, tell their story and the story of their lives as the story of our own—something like Tom Wingo pouring out his heart about his grandfather, certifiably Christian and certifiably crazy.

These incumbent inadequacies are compounded when the story is one of character and morality, a story of the kind of persons people of the way are, or any people are, from a moral point of view. I suspect most of us are stymied when asked to say precisely what a "value" is and where it's grounded, much less get one fully "clarified"; or to render a satisfactory resolution for the latest dilemma in medical, business, or legal ethics; or to provide the prescription for raising a child to be loving, honest, strong, and responsible. With Tom Wingo, what we are most certain of is that the "only word for goodness is goodness, and it is not enough." Powers of understanding, as well as words, ultimately fail.

Nonetheless there is no virtue in being dumb and inarticulate, silent or even hesitant about the people of the way as a community of the gospel and of moral formation and conviction. Resignation is the least helpful of all responses to acculturation and fragmentation. And you can be certain Tom Wingo told Amos stories to his children that they might,

---

[1]Pat Conway, *The Prince of Tides* (Toronto: Bantam Books, 1986) 558–59.

if not know him as he had, at least sense the gospel energy of his blithe spirit in recounting the time at age ninety, on a bet that nearly killed him, he water-skied seventy miles into Hanahan Sound to get his confiscated driver's license back from Patrolman Sasser. So, with a knowing nod to admitted inadequacies, we turn to the faith community and its call to serve as a moral community in this society. The question is, Amid the debris, what treasures still lie at anchor in the blessed harbor of the church's memory? What there will help us learn to "dance in steps of change?"[2]

The Way

I HAVE ALREADY TIPPED MY HAND, WITH THE NAME THE JESUS PEOPLE wore before early onlookers in Antioch tagged them "Christians" forever. Before they were Christians they were "the people of the way." The details are lost to the mists of history, but not entirely so. This was certainly the way of Jesus, himself known as "the Way" by some accounts (John 13:12-20; John 14:5-7; Hebrews 12; 1 Pet. 2:21-24). It was the way of his cross and, both before and after that cataclysm, the way to and in the new age. Only God can create the new age, those first Jesus people knew, yet God presses on the present age to prepare the way; and that preparation was itself already the presence of God's reign in their midst. This life together in God, on this journey with God, was already the Spirit's firstfruits.

Yet for all its early Christian particularity, its origins belong squarely in Judaism with its abiding insistence that the way of God was to be embodied in a way of life by the people of God. Jesus and his people, Israel, were sure of nothing so much as the command to love in deed as they had in deed been loved by the compassionate and righteous One, who, while they were yet slaves, made for them a way where there was none. They were certain that the Ancient of Days had created them as a people in an

[2]The phrase is the title of a book about a congregation in Washington, D.C., The Community of Christ, to which my family belonged for many years and which informs the content of this chapter. The book is clearly dated but it captures the spirit of the early years of the congregation. See David Earle Anderson and John Schramm, *Dancing in Steps of Change* (New York: Thomas Nelson & Sons, 1970). The congregation has the habit of writing its own liturgies out of its common life together. "Dancing in steps of change" is a phrase from one of them.

act of gracious justice and liberation, and that just and gracious relations were to define them as a people of the holy one. The shape of faithfulness to God, they knew in their bones and by aboriginal calling, was to be incarnated in the way of life of a people who had been gathered into covenantal intimacy with none less than Yahweh Sabbaoth, that one God in the crowded pantheon of ancient gods who heard the cries of the poor and knew their suffering. The moral life itself, for Israel and for Jesus, was to witness to this way in a particular pattern of community living; in the instruction and training required for this (discipleship); and in the continuous remembering, retelling, and sacramental reenacting of the formative events by the people of the way themselves. A way of life was to be learned and lived, and it was to be learned and lived together, as the community's own way.

This is not the occasion to remind us that religions typically offer not only cosmic explanations for the powers that bear on us but the manner of life in keeping with such explanations. This is not even the occasion to march the good march up one testament and down the other, to take note of the Deuteronomic choice of the way of life or way of death, blessing or curse; the Sermon on the Mount as instruction in the way; Paul's appeal to his fledgling congregations to "walk a way worthy" of "the God who calls you"; or any number of other traces left so that the faith might have children and the children, faith.

Rather suffice it for the moment to note only that this good Jewish and Christian image refers both to the path itself and the manner of travel. To walk in "the way" as a "people of the way" involves a moral style so intimately related to the destination itself that to wander from the way is also to miss the goal, which is a righteous life in a community faithful to God as "a foretaste of the feast to come."[3] The journey not only tends steadily toward home, the journey itself, to recall Nelle Morton and a hymn, is home.[4] The manner of the route and its travelers is as much a part of the pilgrimage as the final arrival and is in its own way a rehearsal of it. In moral terms, means are themselves "the ends in process" (with thanks to Gandhi for the words and Jesus for the example).

Were there world enough and time, we would say why, in a few

---

[3]A phrase from the Lutheran liturgy.

[4]Nelle Morton, *The Journey Is Home* (Boston: Beacon Press, 1985). Morton took her title from a feminist hymn, "Lead on, O Cloud of Yahweh," with its line, "we are still God's people, the journey is our home." See Prelude, xvii.

short centuries, this first formative metaphor of the Christian life blurred and faded. It never died, nor will it so long as the Jesus story is told and that book which eccentric Amos Wingo sold door-to-door in Colleton County is read with the gravity of faith. The disabling and ultimately tragic development is that the focus soon shifts from Jesus and the particular way he incarnated with his community, the way of his God, to the metaphysical relationship of the individual figure, Jesus, to the church's God, now become also the empire's God. In the most un-Jewish of all possible moves, the Jew Jesus became a "detached" Jesus at the hands of the great ecumenical councils. He was detached from his own historic community and its way, and found himself metaphysically fused to God alone. So one searches in vain in the classic creeds, those pure distillations of the faith, for anything at all about Jesus as the way in any moral sense, or of his community's way.[5]

That Jesus was utterly God-centered is not at issue. It was the whole way of his being. But no pious Jew, including Jesus, would ever understand how anyone in one's very being could be who they are apart from their community and its way. They certainly could not know their God in some other way, for this is the very God who had fashioned their identity as none other than a people of God. The experience of God in Judaism and early Christianity is, first and foremost, the experience of divine

---

[5]In this regard, it is noteworthy that Jürgen Moltmann, in *The Way of Jesus Christ: Christology in Messianic Dimensions* (trans. Margaret Kohl [San Francisco: Harper San Francisco, 1990], 150), suggests that the church add "something along the following lines" to the Nicene and Apostles' creeds, after "born of the Virgin Mary" or "and was made man":

> Baptized by John the Baptist,
> filled with the Holy Spirit:
> to preach the kingdom of God to the poor,
> to heal the sick,
> to receive those who have been cast out,
> to revive Israel for the salvation of the nations, and
> to have mercy upon all people.

Unfortunately, despite Moltmann's efforts to interpret "the way of Jesus Christ" in its Jewishness, he does not, with these suggested additions, make the connection between Jesus' way and his community of disciples. It should be added that the creeds do contain one very important moral element of the way—"the forgiveness of sins." It is ambiguous, however. Is this confession a reference to belief in God's forgiveness of our sins alone, or does it include belief in the forgiveness one of another as a central creedal component of a way of life?

power as the power for peoplehood, and of new creation as community, in, through, and before God. Charlene Spretnak is quite right that while the concentration in Buddhism is on the nature of the serene mind-self, in Native American spirituality on an intimate relationship with nature and the wisdom of its ways, and in Goddess spirituality on honoring the cosmic body, the earth body, and the personal body, the concentration of "the peoples of the Book" (Judaism, Christianity, and Islam) is on community and social justice.[6]

That was largely lost about the time the church's God became the empire's God, however. The church then was no longer a *societas dei* or a *secta dei* (Tertullian) within the bounds of empire, but the empire's own hospital for all sinners. The church was less and less the pre-Constantine pilgrim community, struggling to make community in a world not yet its home, and more and more the empire's standing agent of salvation and its trusty, though often disagreeable, chaplain. With the ecumenical councils as solid history and Christianity established as both the church's faith and the empire's civil religion, the theocentric and communitarian way of Jesus was largely lost. Christianity slipped the long slide from the Pauline revolution in Judaism—the worship of God in Christ—to the worship of (the now detached) Christ as God. As Joseph Sittler notes, the ancient writers' contention that we meet the reality of God in the reality of Jesus is subtly changed to say what they carefully sought to avoid saying—that God and Jesus are an identity.[7] We might well add Sittler's counsel to twentieth-century Christians, that "there is no future in Christians trying to be more Christocentric than Jesus was. And Jesus was not Christocentric at all. His whole life, his words, actions, disposition, and

[6]See Charlene Spretnak, *States of Grace: The Recovery of Meaning in the Postmodern Age* (San Francisco: HarperCollins, 1991).

[7]Joseph Sittler, *Gravity and Grace: Reflections and Provocations* (Minneapolis: Augsburg, 1986), 36–37. The passage begins: "The adoration of God begins not with Christ, but with the one who made heaven and earth. Jesus never called himself Messiah. He did not claim to be God. He claimed to be of God, from God. But he did not claim to be God." It continues: "Look at the language of the Nicene Creed. It does not say 'one substance, but it says being of one substance.' The work in Greek is *ek*—'God from God, light from light, true God from true God.' The ancient writers carefully avoided making an absolute identity. At the same time they denied a chasm in reality between the two. The reality of God meets us in the reality of Jesus. That's a different statement from saying God and Jesus are an identity."

final act were radically theocentric. . . . That whole enormous momentum of the reality of God and the community of faith in God was his fabric and his context."[8] In any event, developments after the ecumenical councils, including the Reformation, only solidified the massive shift from the God-centered Christology of an alternative servant community within the wider world to the Christ-centered theology of a universalizing empire itself. This absorption of virtually all of God into the Jesus of imperial Christianity is at the greatest possible remove from the theocentric Jesus and his yeasty, salty, seed-y community way. Deadly results for Jews, pagans, indigenous peoples and cultures, would eventually follow.

Little wonder that a sensitive Jewish student of Christianity like Franz Rosenzweig says, with a long look at a long history, that the contrast of Christianity with Judaism is that Judaism understands itself as a "way" while Christianity understands itself as a universal community.[9] And little wonder that another great Jewish scholar, Gershom Scholem, contrasts redemption as understood in Judaism with redemption as understood in Christianity on the following lines. Redemption in Judaism is "a process that takes place publicly, on the stage of history and in the medium of the community; in short, which essentially takes place in the visible world, and cannot be thought of except as a phenomenon that appears in what is already visible."[10] Scholem is reiterating the Jewish insistence, from Sinai forward, that concrete historical communal form be given the experience of God's redeeming presence.[11] Against this, Christianity "understands redemption as a happening in the spiritual sphere, and in what is invisible . . . in the soul . . . and in the individual, and effects a mysterious transformation to which nothing external in the world necessarily corresponds."[12] We might well wish to take issue with Scholem's caricature of Christian redemption. Yet it bears enough historical truth to make its case forcefully and reflect that division of labor worked out after Constantine, Theodosius, and Justinian, whereby the

---

[8]Ibid., 106.

[9]See Franz Rosenzweig's discussion in *The Star of Redemption*, trans. W. W. Hallo (Notre Dame and London: Univ. of Notre Dame Press, 1985).

[10]As cited by Jürgen Moltmann in *The Way of Jesus Christ*, 29, from Scholem's "Zum Verständnis der messianischen Idee," *Judaica* (Frankfurt, 1963), 1:7–8.

[11]For a provocative statement of many current themes around this great theme, see Michael Wyschogrod, *The Body of Faith: God in the People Israel* (San Francisco: Harper & Row, 1989).

[12]Scholem, ibid., as cited by Moltmann, *The Way of Jesus Christ*, 29.

church watches over an interiorized notion of salvation and, at least on the face of it, leaves things external to Christian emperors. The church in this scheme looks after souls and their well-being while the emperor claims their bodies and provides for the material welfare and protection of the empire. The marriage of throne and altar and the division of labor were in fact more complex, with church and empire both attending to things material and spiritual, often in collusion, sometimes in conflict. But Scholem's contrast still holds in that Christianity, unlike Judaism, backs away from redemption as a historical reality seen in a visible, communitarian way of life practiced by a distinctive people over time. The larger point, however, is that Scholem's contrast does not hold for earliest Christianity. But that was when the Romans viewed "the people of the way" as a Jewish sect! And as the Jesus movement, that is exactly what those good people were.

Anticipatory Way of Life

WHY SELECT THIS FIRST NAME FOR CHRISTIANS, "THE PEOPLE OF THE way," for a statement on the church as a community of moral conviction in the United States today? That it is hoary with age and experience, carries the honor of the original designation of our people, the people of Jesus, and might itself lead to a fresh way to see ourselves anew would be reason enough. The Reformation principle of *ecclesia reformata, semper reformanda* is always valid: a reformed church is continually in need of further reformation, sparked by returning to its sources with new eyes. But there are additional reasons. They arise from the condition of society described in the foregoing chapters. In fact it is not church scholars but a full passel of sociologists and social critics who say that our season of necessary experimentation in societies around the world requires special attention now to communal enclaves of a certain sort. Not all communal enclaves, but those communities who socialize their members into distinctive, observable ways of life with attention especially to what might be called anticipatory communities. Anticipatory communities are those who work out, in nuts-and-bolts, trial-and-error fashion, ways of life that just might map the ecology of community for greater numbers of people on the far side of a jangled, precarious, extended time of transition. The purpose of such anticipatory communities is to give present social form to a hoped-for future, "thus showing that what might someday be undertaken on a larger scale has already taken recognizable shape" among us.[13] Few things, claim these watchers of uncertain society, are more helpful than disciplined communities who offer plausible and meaningful ways of life together in largely noncoercive ways. Such communities usually inhabit society's margins, at least at the outset, and usually gather their membership from those who are not, or do not feel, most heavily invested in prominent and dominant structures and ways. Their lifeblood and their ways are, in different words, less invested in the institutions of modernity now creaking in the beams.

What Ernst Troeltsch noted about the dynamics of the Jesus people of the way and of periodic church renewal movements can be generalized here.[14] Two forces come together for societal renewal. One is the development of community-creating religion among lower socioeconomic classes, among other marginalized groups, and among the disaffected from the ranks of the socially privileged. Here, whether in separate communities or together, an urgent sense of clear, stark, human need is joined to a faith full of feeling, energy, clear conviction, and direction. Divine power is experienced anew as the power for peoplehood and for making a way where there was none. The other movement is the conceptual and ritual revisioning of inherited traditions in times of deep, bewildering, and sometimes frightening and dangerous change. Criticism that rings true, bold theological review, and constructive exploration in thought and in liturgical enactment are trademarks here. When these movements come together, new religious vitalities are loosed upon the world. The outcome is never clean, to be sure. It is conflicted the way things human always are. It draws the crazy likes of Amos Wingo and Amos the prophet. But communities and ways of life are forged and refined in such crucibles, and occasionally the wider world awakens one morning to find instrumentalities it didn't remember molding. Or if it did, didn't expect in this form.[15]

At this juncture, and for reasons best explained by short-circuiting in the brain, remarks by Margaret Mead, John Yoder, Cornel West, and

---

[13]Bruce C. Birch and Larry L. Rasmussen, *The Predicament of the Prosperous* (Philadelphia: Westminster Press, 1978), 191.

[14]See Ernst Troeltsch's discussion in *The Social Teaching of the Christian Churches*, vol. 2 (Chicago and London: University of Chicago Press, 1981), esp. 43–46.

[15]See Larry Rasmussen, "New Dynamics in Theology: Politically Active and Culturally Significant," in *Ethics in the Present Tense*, ed. Leon Howell and Vivian Lindermayer (New York: Friendship Press, 1991), 55–65.

Vincent Harding all jump to mind at once. Margaret Mead's is: "Never doubt that a small group of thoughtful committed citizens can change the world; indeed it's the only thing that ever has." The word *only* in that sentence need not be defended in order to affirm the rest. John Yoder's is in the same key but in two parts. First he remarks about Jesus choosing the disciples (Luke 6:12ff.). "To organized opposition [Jesus] responds with the formal founding of a new social reality. New teachings are no threat, as long as the teacher stands alone; a movement, extending his personality in both time and space, presenting an alternative to the structures that were there before, challenges the system as no mere words could."[16]

Later Yoder observes this about the social reality Jesus has gathered around him.

> There are . . . thus about the community of disciples those sociological traits most characteristic of those who set about to change society: a visible structured fellowship, a sober decision guaranteeing that the costs of commitment to the fellowship have been consciously accepted, and a clearly defined life style distinct from that of the crowd. This life style is different, not because of arbitrary rules separating the believer's behavior from that of "normal people," but because of the exceptionally normal quality of humanness to which the community is committed. The distinctness is not a cultic or ritual separation, but rather a nonconformed quality of ("secular") involvement in the life of the world. It thereby constitutes an unavoidable challenge to the powers that be and the beginning of a new set of social alternatives.[17]

I cite Vincent Harding's response to *Habits of the Heart* and Cornel West's to *The Good Society*. Harding's eloquent epistle, "Toward a Darkly Radiant Vision of America's Truth: A Letter of Concern, an Invitation to Re-Creation," first notes that the attention of *Habits of the Heart* to white, middle-class Americans only meant, in the authors' own words, that "we were not able to illustrate much of the racial diversity

---

[16]John Howard Yoder, *The Politics of Jesus* (Grand Rapids, Mich.: Wm. B. Eerdmans, 1972), 40.
[17]Ibid., 46–47.

that is so important a part of our national life."[18] Harding replies that this absence was not, as such, the primary loss. Rather what is missing "is a major portion of the painful reality, the ambiguous richness, and the anguished integrity of this nation's past and present—as well as a full sense of the magnificent possibilities of its future."[19] Not to move outside the cultural experience and sense of history of most white middle-strata Americans is to bypass, forsake, or ignore the treasures amid the pain in "one of the most fascinating and frustratingly multicultural nations in the world."[20] For a large, provincial nation in a wildly multicultural, multiracial, and multireligious world, that makes no sense whatsoever, especially when the agenda is society's moral renewal in the naked public square. What is at stake is fashioning some viable alternative(s) to modernity's deadliness and postmodernity's aimlessless.

Cornel West's review of *The Good Society*, aptly titled "The Struggle for America's Soul," includes the following:

> The book suggests that perhaps "a new social movement is called for," yet the authors do not tell us who will constitute this movement. They know it must be a multiracial affair, but they give us no clue as to how this coming together can take place, or what will hold such a movement together.
>
> The moral vision of the authors is commendable, their motives noble, their analysis subtle. Yet their prophetic jeremiad is slightly out of touch with the inchoate, scattered yet gathering progressive movement that is emerging across the American landscape. This gathering now lacks both the vital moral vocabulary and the focused leadership that can constitute and sustain it. Yet it will be rooted ultimately in current activities by people of color, by labor and ecological groups, by women, by homosexuals. These activities do not receive serious examination in this book.[21]

---

[18]Robert Bellah et al., *Habits of the Heart* (Berkeley and Los Angeles: University of California Press, 1985), viii.

[19]Vincent Harding, "Toward a Darkly Radiant Vision of America's Truth: A Letter of Concern, An Invitation to Re-Creation," in *Community in America*, ed. Charles H. Reynolds and Ralph V. Norman (Berkeley, Los Angeles, London: University of California Press, 1988), 68.

[20]Ibid.

[21]Cornel West, "The Struggle for America's Soul," *New York Times Book Review*,

How will "this coming together take place," these treasures of "one of the most fascinating and frustratingly multicultural and multiracial nations in the world" be uncovered and paraded? Who will answer the call to advance "the vital moral vocabulary" and step forward with "the focused leadership"? What band of disciples will consider the costs and take the pledge? What moral communities will try noncoercively to offer, in an unwilling world, the order to come? What communities will gather the peoples of the inchoate margins and, with them and the dissenting center, dream and organize in rituals and other deeds a gracious way of life that demands no more than that it be considered a very serious and joyous matter? Where are the moral communities for this? Will they take the plunge? Are the churches among them? History has as much need of these communities as it has of any.

We have lamented here, though still an octave less shrill than Jeremiah, or even Isaiah, that our culture's atomization of moral community is so far advanced we have no more hope for vibrant communities of moral formation and conviction than the hope of a smoldering wick or a bruised reed. In fact the horizon is thicker with promise than that. It is more promising because some signs indicate that the churches are shucking the remnants of a European and U.S. cultural Christianity complex and remembering that we (I mean we Christians) were a multicultural and multiracial people drawn from many lands long, long before 1492. There are a few signs that we do not forget our ancestors when they die or the globe-encompassing identity they tendered to us through countless generations from those hazy beginnings centuries ago somewhere near Ur of the Chaldees.

In addition to that expanded sense of ecumenical identity, there are also a few converging "secular" signs. Even among the most privatized followers of religion in the U.S. there seems to be developing a more public language of social and moral responsiveness. Some of it speaks the language of "healing" but moves more toward community healing. Some of it rallies around environmental concern and "healing the planet." Some of it simply will no longer tolerate the violations that attend homelessness, child and spouse abuse, and race and class destructiveness. Some of it has caught the vision of the progressive gathering West sees beginning to happen and Harding knows by its treasures.

---

15 September 1991, 13.

However fragile the reed and imperiled the wick, hope stirs and will not be defeated.

Still, the scattered soul of this society awaits communities of moral conviction and leadership with identities and memories that know the strengths of a longer past than the scattered soul knows; communities that also, by faith, know a longer, more hopeful future. It awaits these same communities as ones who also relish some holy hilarity along the way.

But what shall we say about the church as such a community? The acculturation of middle-American churches is too advanced to expect any coherent mass movement. The attention, then, is to those church communities, limited in number, who will risk venture on this way. We can post the specific roles these churches are called to as this kind of community. In the discipline of Christian ethics, "roles" move between factual descriptions of social situations and moral responses about what ought to be done amid them.[22] In our case they help answer questions of the churches' public moral calling during a season of forced experimentation, a season that at the same time calls for the renewal of society's moral fiber. Readers should permit themselves some dreaming. If Jeremiah could buy up a little patch of real estate in Babylon and settle down to some serious dreaming, so can we.

Timely Roles

"FEMINIST MORAL THEOLOGY," BEVERLY HARRISON WRITES, "IS UTOPIAN, as all good theology is, in that it *envisages* a society, a world, a cosmos, in which . . . there are 'no excluded ones.'"[23] This is the church's universal, or catholic, vision and conviction—the necessary, full inclusion of the excluded, on egalitarian terms, as children of God all.

Universalism and egalitarianism are both important. Both are assertions of faith itself, whether or not they also have secular grounds. The contention is that God takes a compassionate and unwearying high interest in each human being, indeed in all creation. "The Christian universe is peopled exclusively with royalty," says Glenn Tinder, echoing

---

[22]The single best discussion of roles from a moral point of view may still be Dorothy Emmet's in *Rules, Roles and Relations* (Boston: Beacon Press, 1966).

[23]Beverly Wildung Harrison, *Making the Connections: Essays in Feminist Social Ethics*, ed. Carol S. Robb (Boston: Beacon Press, 1985), 20, quoting Jules Girardi.

Luther.[24] For life in community it means that all deserve attention and an unexceptionable rule that "*no one* is to be casually sacrificed."[25] Each person has been immeasurably dignified by God. No one is an alien and barbarian or belongs at the bottom.[26] Nor dare any be consigned to silence or deprived of those powers that mean full participation as members of the community. For a people of the way, faith doesn't make distinctions that violate this basic equality and universalism. The community's life is fashioned in keeping with it.

Here is the converging Christian ground for one of the lasting moral achievements of modernity itself—universal human rights. Persons are to be cared for when they are destitute or cannot care for themselves, respected and listened to when they gather and speak, accorded privacy by government when they do not break the law, and treated and tried fairly when they do.[27] The churches' case embracing rights and for democratic participation rests in its vision of a society in which membership is on egalitarian terms and there are no excluded ones. God's love and grace exalts all. All have intrinsic value as God's creatures. All are sacred whether or not any are good.[28]

What does this mean for the community's own day-to-day, year-to-year transactions, whether or not parallels exist in the wider society? It means for us, as it meant for Jesus and the people of the way, living as if, as if God's exalting, leveling grace and its way mattered. It means living as if the barriers between rich, poor, and underclass were not the givens the present economy says they are; living as if the chief actor of the past two hundred years, the nation-state, were no longer the only chief power, since it is now too large for local problems and too small for global ones; living as if the world were indeed a single public household or world house, to recall Martin Luther King's image; or, in another of his images, living as if we constituted a single moral community wrapped in a common garment and shared destiny. What better moral leadership could the church offer than to become genuinely ecumenical and, as a habit of mind, heart, and hands, live as if the entire planet's fecund variety were all part of the same covenantal intimacy it knows in

---

[24]Glenn Tinder, "Can We Be Good Without God?" *Atlantic Monthly*, December 1989, 72.
[25]Ibid.
[26]Ibid.
[27]Ibid.
[28]Ibid., 76.

God? What notion of "public" could be more helpful than one mirroring a society where all belong, sharing the same loaf and drinking from the same cup, occupying a common earthspace, and parceling and replenishing the same resources? We are in fact already bundled together in a common fate in a contracting world of heightened cumulative human power. So what community could contribute more than one that showed how to share more egalitarian ways of life together? Or what community could contribute more than one that was a genuine sanctuary, a sacred and safe place where the deepest differences could be drawn on and the most controversial issues deliberated together?

Few communities are better poised geographically or by virtue of their vocation. Spin the globe and stab your finger to stop it and you probably put your first digit through the roof of somebody's church somewhere. When we most need institutions that are as local as the neighborhood and as global as the planet itself, we have at least one transnational body already on the job whose very calling it is to gather all, on equal terms, into caring community across barriers that divide. According to Ephesians 2 and the Jesus movement itself, that is precisely when and how, through Jesus's cross, "church" happens.

This kind of community mirrors the audacity of the early church and its faith. Small, cell-like as it was, it understood membership as dynamically creating a third race, a new humanity from estranged peoples. Jews and Gentiles, slaves and free, men and women—this slice across the *oikoumenē* (the whole inhabited world) would together fashion a new way as a community gathered in God. "Global" membership, drawn from every land and people and living together on equal terms, was the early ecumenical dream of human unity and peace.

It did not last long. The separation of synagogue and church among the early Christians sabotaged its precarious beginnings, while its "realization" as a universal community in the form of Christendom undid it on a grand scale through the corruption of imperial power married to an imperial faith. A noncoerced version, with only the weapons of the weak and far more modesty, remains the dream nonetheless. And while both form and substance must be different, a vocation today continues for noncoerced global communities whose life is in the Spirit and whose morality works to overcome dividing differences through shared and equal power.

The church as an inclusive moral community is well poised for another reason, beyond the fact of its global net and its vocation, or ministry, of reconciliation. It is the task of religious communities as such to give leadership in matters of cosmology and ethics. They are expected to reply to the queries of heart and mind postmodern confusion throws up: Who and where are we in the scheme of things, anyway? Where are we going, and what does it mean? Is there bread for the journey? What is the way of life appropriate to the coming age? Where do we muster the courage to live it? These are the intensely practical, spiritual, and moral questions millions ask, either forthrightly or as inarticulate groanings of the spirit. Religious communities have some practice here. A catholic one of myriad voices and traditions has some treasures to unpack and others yet to discover. None of this is done facilely or without pain. But if it is done together, as it often has been in the course of a shared history, it can fund experience and offer wisdom. With God's grace, that suffices to take up the moral and cosmological tasks anew.

There is another dimension of community and cosmology that may be genuinely new and that can be nurtured by communities of inclusive membership. Although it is true that "no one can be universal anywhere except in his [or her] own backyard," to remember a line from de Mores,[29] and we are forever stuck with our finitude, the human venture has always found it extraordinarily difficult to cross the barriers that divide peoples into us and them, into ourselves and alien others. Efforts at genuine world citizenship seem always to crash on the same shoals where other ideals have run aground, the shoals of an identity too large and demanding for our rooted, culturebound selves to embrace. Caught in our own cultural autism, our moral imaginations never fully break through to take in others in a common but extraordinarily diverse membership.

Yet the first light of a fresh dawn may silently slice through a cracked doorway now. The light is as silent as the image of this marbled planet taken from space. This image is itself a symbol of religious power for millions. It reinforces the postmodern "reenchantment of the world" as a community of sacred subjects, which indigenous peoples have known in their bones and psyches for centuries. It calls up anew the most primordial of all visions—namely, that person and community and community and cosmos are inseparable and mutually reinforcing and enhancing.[30]

---

[29]Vincinius de Mores, as cited by Rubem Alves in *Tomorrow's Child: Imagination, Creativity and the Rebirth of Culture* (New York: Harper & Row, 1972), 182.

[30]See the very fine chapter by Carol Johnston, "Economics, Eco-justice, and the Doctrine of God," in *After Nature's Revolt*, ed. Dieter Hessel (Minneapolis: Fortress Press, 1992), 154–70. The sentence just noted is adapted from her discussion,

The promise it bears is that we may at last be able to understand ourselves as citizens of a world without borders.

Such a shift in cosmological thinking does not occur by the power of a compelling vision alone, however, or by way of lauded paradigm shifts. These are not enough. The hard push of grave survival threats may be enough, however, when they combine with that vision without which the people perish. Already agonies that know no borders have forced unprecedented international cooperation and have called into question modernity's hoarding of soverignty by nation-states. The cries of the earth rise to heaven and on the way begin to open deaf human ears. For a community whose very first article of faith is a confession of God as the Creator of a good creation, and whose vision has been that of all creation redeemed to its fullest possible flourishing, this moment is a reply to an extraordinary invitation and an ancient hope. The invitation is to meld the possibilities of our necessarily modest times and places with the reality of planetary citizenship. Community on such a scale may not be possible—a most unbiblical and unhopeful conclusion!—but it is necessary. For a community that is catholic by calling, all this is more than reason enough.

This kind of universal community, to recall Rosenzweig's tentative attraction to a chastened Christianity, is the kind that now might be the Christian gift and treasure. It must be amended that this would be in sharpest contrast with "universal" as the tag for various marriages of throne and altar that have blessed so many Christian imperial adventures, including some modern democratic capitalist ones. Of course, those were never universal at all, but only large sects still living from more or less Manichaean us's and thems, insiders and outsiders, the saved and the damned (or at least the unevangelized). As an egalitarian community, this universal community is also in sharpest contrast to churches and other communities in U.S. society that perpetuate culturally and economically embedded forms of domination and discrimination, thereby forever setting people against one another along lines of race, class, ethnic difference, gender, age, or physical ability. A catholic moral vision means that dividing walls, like the Berlin Wall itself, must fall.

Even irrepressible dreamers know that nothing is ever real until it is embodied, however. What counts with God and one another is not "opportunity," or even vision, but incarnation. What carries power and

---

164–65.

promise and generates conviction and courage is concrete community. So we must speak of moral leadership in the form of the church as a community of "pioneering creativity" (John Yoder). Very practical theological and technical attention must be given to what the churches do with their own institutional property and moneys, for example, and what they commend to members about theirs, how they are earned, invested, spent, and otherwise distributed. It means attending to how governance happens in these ranks, the quality of our treatment of one another within the household of faith, the mirroring of the vision of inclusive, egalitarian membership in each locale. It means attending to the way the earth and things of the earth are cared for in this open enclave of creation.

Luther, for whom evangelical freedom did not mean vague living, may have been too exacting in his recommended range of community judgments. But he is right that a way of life turns on the little things as well as the grand, on the everyday as well as the extraordinary. "The church," he wrote, "is the pupil of Christ, sitting at his feet and hearing his Word so that she may know how to pass judgment on everything, how to serve in one's calling, how to adminster public offices, aye, also how to eat, drink, and sleep, that there may be no doubt about the proper conduct in any walk of life but, surrounded on all sides by the Word of God, one may constantly walk in joy and in the light."[31]

We should not make little of the potential power of this joyous walk as a way of life. It is, to shift images, the power of a seed. So very often the moral soundness of the world beyond the church is served best by faith communities that live out that moral soundness in the detail of their own ranks. In a season of "forced options"[32] and exploration, because the world is caught in the throes of everything at once, this pioneering creativity by voluntary organizations with strong membership loyalties is particularly well poised to sow seeds—mustard seeds, to be precise.

George Lindbeck's comment might be added: "Religious communities are likely to be practically relevant in the long run to the degree that

---

[31]Martin Luther, as cited by Herbert Brokering and Roland Bainton, *Luther's Germany* (Minneapolis: Augsburg, 1985), 51.

[32]The reference is to Roger Lincoln Shinn, *Forced Options: Social Decisions for the Twenty-first Century*, (Cleveland: Pilgrim Press, 1991). The phrase, as Shinn explains, is one taken from William James and refers to social choices that allow no escape. The whole of the book is relevant to our concerns, but see esp. the opening discussion of how societies decide, and the discussions in part 3 on pervasive, intertwined social, ethical, and religious issues.

they do not first ask what is either practical or relevant, but instead concentrate on their own intratextual outlooks and forms of life."[33] That is, faithfulness and a communal way of life in accord with it is often the most effective strategy even when it is never plotted as such. Lindbeck continues with an insightful Lutheran twist: "The much-debated problem of the relation of theory and praxis is thus dissolved by the communal analogue of justification by faith. As is true for individuals, so also a religious community's salvation is not by works, nor is faith for the sake of practical efficacy, and yet good works of unforeseeable kinds flow from faithfulness."[34]

"Pioneering creativity" must be broadened to speak of "practices," a matter of much attention in recent Christian ethics and social theory. Practices are indispensable to moral formation. But what precisely are they and how do they function morally?

"Practices" is not simply a synonym for "actions," as though anything we might do, if repeated a few times and worked up as a routine, would constitute a practice. Practices are those particularly pregnant actions that are "both a means to a good life and also aspects of a historically constituted good form of life."[35] They are focal actions,[36] to recall Borgmann. *Focus*, the Latin word for "hearth," was the center of the household in Roman times. It was not only the place where the family gathered for warmth and food but the common holy place where the household gods resided, where marriages were sanctified, and where festal celebrations occurred. The hearth (in contrast to the central heating unit!) was that around which daily life was centered, sustained, ordered. "Focal practices," then, are those actions intrinsic to a way of life that center, sustain, and order that way of living. They are common to life and precious, recurrent, and significant. They are not simply experiences or events that temporarily light up our life like a good song. They are the engaging, reenacted actions of a certain ritual quality, if not always a

---

[33]Lindbeck, *The Nature of Doctrine: Religion and Theology in a Postliberal Age* (Philadelphia: Westminster Press, 1984), 128.
[34]Ibid.
[35]Bellah et al., *The Good Society* (New York: Alfred A. Knopf, 1991), 290, drawing on Alasdair MacIntyre's discussion of practices in *After Virtue* (Notre Dame: University of Notre Dame Press, 1981).
[36]See Borgmann's discussion, *Technology and the Character of Contemporary Life: A Philosophical Inquiry* (Chicago: University of Chicago Press, 1984), 196ff.

ritual format. In all this they show the way. They perform the faith as a way of life. They are rites that embody what is right.

Take hospitality, for example. Preparing a meal with love and care and spice, enjoying the presence of one another in good conversation at the table and afterward over coffee, and showing the welcomed guests to quarters that, while modest, reflect your sincere desire for their comfort—all this is far more than the minimum daily requirement of calories and required rest. It is a deliberate, ritualized, recurrent action, complete with gesture and nuance and part of "a constituted good form of life," part of a way of life in community. "We invite each other not to eat and drink," Plutarch once remarked, "but to eat and drink together."[37]

The meal together may have been a reunion with old friends and the making of some new ones. It may have gathered people scattered across forbidding distances. It may have recollected and reenacted an old tradition or inaugurated a new one. It may have been the occasion to see a different side to someone well known. It may have been the time to try a new recipe or add a special course, postponed until just the right occasion. It may have been the moment for a special prayer of thanks to God for the delectable produce of nature and the company of friends from other cultures. It may have been the occasion to toast the newest member of this extemporaneous family, salute a new partnership, or comfort the newly widowed. This is hospitality partaking of a practice.[38] A TV dinner does not.

---

[37]As cited by Christopher Idone in "What's Coming Up?" *New York Times Magazine*, 29 December 1991, sect. 6, p. 31.

[38]Hospitality is, of course, a strong biblical theme from the earliest strata of the Hebrew Bible. It continued in early Christian traditions. One ancient one, a Celtic rune of hospitality, catches the biblical tone itself well.

> We saw a stranger yesterday.
> We put food in the eating place.
> Drink in the drinking place.
> Music in the listening place.
> And with the sacred name of the Triune God
> He blessed our house.
> Our cattle and our dear ones.
>
> As the lark says in her song;
> Often, often, often goes the Christ in the stranger's guise.

From an anonymous author, "Old Celtic Rune," adapted in *The Iona Community Worship Book* and cited by Johanna H. Young, "Waters of the Well: A Christian Response to Water in Peril" (Master's thesis, Union Theological Seminary, New

In short, practices are those actions that belong to a way of life as means to appropriate ends (eating, resting); are worthy ends in their own right (breaking bread together, the communion of hospitality); and are the mediums whereby our lives are centered, ordered, and sustained.

The forms of practices are many, from highly ritualized ceremonies to the informality of half-noticed routines (a handshake, a greeting). The faith community's sacraments, as rich, carefully ritualized reenactments, are on one end of this spectrum. Yet sacraments are practices supreme only if and when they embody and show forth their connectedness to the rest of life, only if and when they "show the way." Bread, to continue the example of food, is the staff of life, the body of Christ, the symbol of the Sabbath, and a means of livelihood, hospitality, and eucharistic companionship.[39] For Christians, the Supper of the Lamb is a central and centering event. It recalls the gathering of a new community and the inclusion of the excluded in that decisive act of Jesus, his eating "with outcasts and sinners" in a new table community that included all and dissolved their social differences. It recalls the meal of Jesus' death with his disciples and, within that canonical narrative, the Seder meal and Passover liberation. It recollects the resurrection appearances and the recognition of Jesus "in the breaking of bread." It remembers that in the ancient Mediterranean any notion of the kingdom of heaven had to have something to do with eating and drinking and feasting together, and that the reign of God would finally show itself as a lavish messianic banquet. It returns anew to the catholic dream for church and world repeated in the measured phrases of the ancient *Didache*: "As this broken bread was scattered upon the mountains, and being gathered together became one, so may your church be gathered together from the ends of the earth into your kingdom."[40]

When the ritual reenactment of this sharing of food is part of a way of life that takes in the rest of life, and focuses our everyday hopes and actions, then the sacrament has again become a focal practice with the power of its origins. It is this when, for example, it breaks down the barriers between races, classes, gender, and culture by welcoming all to the

York, 1992), 39.

[39]Michael Walzer, *Spheres of Justice* (New York: Basic Books, 1983), 8.

[40]The *Didache* as cited by Konrad Raiser, *Ecumenism in Transition* (Geneva: WCC Publications, 1991), 98.

welcome table; when it connects with the many hungers of the world, including malnutrition and starvation, and moves people to alleviate them as best they can; when it celebrates the blessed creation in gratitude for life itself and recognizes God in, with, and under simple, ordinary things like wheat and the fruit of the vine; when it brings judgment and a call to repentance to all the tables where the stranger is not welcomed as a partner; and when it means new beginnings for a forgiven and refreshed people around an inclusive table community. Then the Eucharist is once again a practice supreme.[41]

Or one might recollect Saturday night and third-century baptism in North Africa. Those taking instruction, normally over two years, started out as "beginners" (*rudes*) but soon became "catechumens." The Greek root of catechumen is *echo*, since the catechumens were to "echo" in their own lives the conduct they learned of by way of instruction in the Christian life. This instruction was their prebaptismal moral formation.[42] When the period of catechetical instruction drew to an end, and baptism and Easter approached, the catechumens became "competents." Competency was a time for testing and all manner of rites, some of them strange to us—exorcisms, unceasing prayer, generous oil anointings. Competency demonstrated, they heard the baptismal creed confided by the bishop on the Saturday fifteen days before Easter. Saturday night a week later they began a set of rites that continued through Holy Week and that interwove actions of all kinds (lamplighting, foot washing, bathing, fast-

---

[41]In my office I have a copy of Andrey Rublev's icon of the Trinity. The hospitality shown by Abraham to the three strangers (Gen. 18:1–8) is in this icon a symbol of the dwelling of the triune God in God's house around the eucharistic meal. Konrad Raiser (*Ecumenism in Transition*, III) includes this commentary on this Orthodox icon:

> The cup, which in the Orthodox tradition contains both the bread and the wine, is the central message of this icon for the life of the world. The lack of daily bread, for which Christ taught us to pray, brings hunger, starvation and death to a world that is now unjustly divided between the rich and the poor. Here is the meeting of ecumenics and economics. The eucharistic cup calls for a daily sharing of bread and of material and spiritual resources with the millions of hungry people in this world. Through them God, the Trinity, comes on pilgrimage to us at every moment.

[42]Thomas M. Finn, "It Happened One Saturday Night: Ritual and Conversion in Augustine's North Africa," *Journal of the American Academy of Religion* 58, 4: 590.

ing) with prayers, psalmody, homilies, and instruction on the challenge of conversion for day-to-day conduct as new members of the family of God.

The "sublime nightwatch" happened the Saturday night before Easter and lasted from sunset until sunrise, when the baptismal rite itself was celebrated and the competents could finally, after two years, participate firsthand in the great mysteries of the faith. The baptismal water consecrated, the competents processed to the font, took off their garments of simple "penitential" cloth, responded to a final inquiry about their faith, and were immersed three times in the name of the Holy Trinity. The bishop anointed them with oil, made the sign of the cross on their foreheads, and gave them the garment of new life, woven of white linen. They received the baptismal candle and the embrace of the congregation, followed by the celebration of their very first Eucharist.[43]

The details of the rites are elaborate, fascinating, and worthy of study. We cannot entertain them here, except to note that they included standing and facing Rome to "renounce the devil and all his works and all his ways" and turning toward Jerusalem to confess the faith one would now walk by. Baptism was a declaration of "no" to one way of life and "yes" to another, a schooling in the latter, and a ritual enactment of it. It was, in its own language, both *aversio* and *conversio*, a turning from and a turning to. What was turned to was the religiously formed way of life that membership in this primary community entailed. What was turned from was the "worldly" way of life signaled by imperial Rome.[44] Thomas Finn, who passes this along in great detail, concludes that "the first thing the rites disclose is that the task of conversion was to reshape an entire way of living and system of values," and that "the community . . . was an encircling presence in all the rites." Indeed the community was itself "renewed in the rites" as members joined the competents at

[43]Ibid., 593–94.

[44]An even more basic set of symbols was involved with this. Turning to Jerusalem means facing east and the rising of the sun. Turning toward Rome meant west and encroaching darkness. Whether the geography was always accurate or not, day and night, light and darkness reinforced the dualist conviction of the early church that a contrasting way of life was entailed, what the second-century *Didache* profiles as "the path of life" and "the path of death." (See "The Didache: Instruction of the Lord to the Gentiles" in Jan L. Womer, ed., *Morality and Ethics in Early Christianity* [Minneapolis: Fortress Press, 1987], 30–33.)

every stage in this elaborate journey.[45] This is baptism as a focal practice. The connections from center outward were made, and moral character was formed and reformed around this center. A way of life was ordered and sustained in a ritual performance of its faith.

A living community imaginatively renews such living traditions as practices for its own time and place. We might consider, for example, carrying out the ancient baptismal rite in the toxic waters of some factory stream in our neighborhood, preferably a factory in which congregation members have work and on which the neighborhood depends. What would the "living waters" that flow from the throne of God (Revelation 22) mean for our collective way of life with such a baptism? What moral convictions would be engendered, and what kind of character shaped? What concrete shape might the faith of the congregation take? Would it insist on pure water for baptism? What would that say about responsibility for the neighborhood's water? Either way—with pure water or toxic—such a baptism might testify powerfully to James Baldwin's words even when he did not intend them for the church: "One cannot allow oneself, nor can one's family, friends, or lovers—to say nothing of one's children—to live according to the world's definitions: one must find a way, perpetually, to be stronger and better than that."[46]

Communities of pioneering creativity display practices (to return to the main discussion from this aside on sacraments as practices). What practices do is about means, ends, "ordering" actions, and the way of life that connects them all internally. Of course other actions of the community also entail practices. Sacraments are only the most intensely ritualized. The important matter is the nature and function of practices themselves and the preserving, transforming, and creative dimensions of their formal or informal ritual performance.[47]

---

[45]Finn, "It Happened One Saturday Night," 609–10.

[46]Baldwin's words are quoted as the frontispiece of John Stoltenberg's *Refusing to Be a Man: Essays on Sex and Justice* (New York: Meridian, 1989).

[47]Unfortunately we cannot here carry on a discussion of the important insights from ritual studies. But readers should know of the outstanding volume by Tom F. Driver, *The Magic of Ritual: Our Need for Liberating Rites that Transform Our Lives and Our Communities* (San Francisco: Harper San Francisco, 1991). Especially helpful to our discussion of practices and a religiously formed way of life is the chapter "Ritual's Two Siblings: Performance in the Confessional and the Ethical Modes," 107–30.

What does this mean for moral formation in our society? That is the question at hand. Fortunately it is easy to answer. As moral development educators have long known, we learn moral ways through practices. By assuming roles, by becoming familiar with exemplary behavior and the guiding narratives of a way of life, by joining with the typical characters who live it (like Tom Wingo tagging along with Amos), and by being part of its ritualistic observances, we become the kinds of persons we are.[48] Differently said, by becoming self-involved and self-invested in the patterns of a way of life as carried out in community practices, our character is formed and life is given a shape. Practices answer the question, what is the best way of life for us to lead?

It is important to add that the whole way of life educates and forms, not the episodic observances sometimes mistaken for practices (attending church on high holy days only, for example, or giving thanks together only on Thanksgiving). Practices are not practices unless they are the connective tissue in a whole way of life that *in toto* steadily shapes the participants. Practices are elements of "praxis," or practice as the concrete, lived way of life. And virtue, indeed the moral life as a whole, replete with obligations, values, and vision, conforms to praxis.[49]

Thus are practices, and a people of the way, powerful. Perhaps little else finally is, since coerced relationships often indulge the bad habit of doing themselves in through the spiral of resentment, recrimination, violence, and counterviolence. Better to use the weapons of the weak, as did the first people of the way—other-regarding morality (the community, not the individual self, is the primary moral unit); a "subversive" memory; projection of a powerful vision; the presence of persons of such integrity and depth they will extend themselves to the point of sacrifice, even risking death, to live toward the vision and keep faith with the remembered; a set of alternative institutions (the black church in the civil

---

[48]Though he is a philosopher and not a psychologist of moral development, Alaisdair MacIntyre merits attention for his discussions of practices and the moral life. See esp. *After Virtue* 2d ed. (Notre Dame and London: Univ. of Notre Dame Press, 1984) and *Three Rival Versions of Moral Inquiry: Encyclopedia, Genealogy and Tradition* (Notre Dame and London: Univ. of Notre Dame Press, 1991).

[49]See the discussion by Sheila Briggs of the church as a community of practice in Willis H. Logan, ed., *The Kairos Covenant* (New York: Meyer-Stone Books and Friendship Press, 1988), 80–94. For an important discussion of the generative nature of practice for the substance of thought and perspective, see Sara Ruddick, *Maternal Thinking: Toward a Politics of Peace* (Boston: Beacon Press, 1989).

rights movement, for example, or underground Polish cultural and educational institutions during decades of occupation); and an ability, when conditions permit, to leverage even towering institutions. (The role of Roman Catholic women's religious orders in the Interfaith Center for Corporate Responsibility has, with other church groups, brought pressures for social responsibility to bear on corporations just as it has given a new form of witness to the orders themselves and strengthened them as moral agents within the Roman church.) In any event, effective communities of creativity are those that have an almost sacramental respect for what they do and are patient to teach and share that which belongs to "a way." They know that the moral life means mentoring and crafting and takes time.

The focal practices of a way are as subject to moral judgment as any other and always in need of interrogation about their moral quality. Practices, we must underscore, have only prima facie moral worth. The generation of moral community requires them, but their specific content and consequences must be assessed. Thus a set of questions is entailed. What, precisely, is being communicated about a way of life in these practices? Who is included and who is not? What do they imply for other dimensions of our lives? How does this way compare and contrast with others in the world around us? What kind of community do these practices form? What shake down as the vital values, virtues, obligations? What is the moral vision of this way of life as it manifests itself? What do subscribers to this way of life understand as their circle of responsibility and accountability? In the faith community, then, an exegesis of praxis and practices should be on a par with the exegesis of the canonical texts and traditions, and connected with each other.[50] Special attention should

[50]Stephen E. Fowl and L. Gregory Jones, in *Reading in Communion: Scripture and Ethics in Christian Life* (Grand Rapids, Mich.: Wm. B. Eerdmans, 1991), are good on this and many other points. Their discussion of Birch and Rasmussen, *Bible and Ethics in the Christian Life*, is thus all the more baffling. After saying that it and Thomas Ogletree's *Use of the Bible in Christian Ethics* "attend both to the formation of character and the importance of community" (9), they go on to speak of "a preoccupation with decisions made by individuals" that "continues to shape both books" (ibid.). They also contend that the discussion of character puts it "alongside such other elements as rules, principles, values and assessments of consequences" (10). Whatever the case for Ogletree, this is a very serious misreading of Birch and Rasmussen. Our entire volume in its second edition places character and decision making within an organization of materials around the

always be given the power relationships that praxis and practices reflect and their shape in the church community. The same can be said for the moral analysis the community does of the canons, praxis, and practices it finds in the culture around it. Cultures and subcultures are ways of life subject to this same analysis.

"Pioneering creativity" refers to even more than community moral formation through practices, however. In the modern-postmodern season of transition, it also means experimentation with community itself. As noted earlier, we have no desire for or need of the traditional communities of premodern homogeneity and rule. Only reactionary romanticism lies down that path, with its propensity to foist on nature or the Deity those arrangements for which human beings are responsible. Rather we need full human responsibility not only for sounder communities of intimacy (family and neighborhood communities, in the first instance) but for communities that combine communitarian ties and associational ones. These are communities that draw on the positive moral capital of modernity itself (freedom, genuine democratic participation, equal rights guaranteed by law) and that welcome strangers. At their best, they provide a community ethos for modernity's interdependent strangers so as to make common cause together around a meaningful collective identity. In some instances (churches and other religious communities, for example), they may even fashion a people and a way from the ranks of strangers become close community. In any event, our kind of world calls for pioneering creativity in the form of promoting communities with those practices that gather strangers together to share a common space, membership, and purpose.

The two aforementioned roles—inclusive, egalitarian membership

---

themes of community and moral agency. The discussion of moral virtue, value, obligation, and vision is itself located within this framework and as a part of the discussion of character and decision making. The chapter on decision making itself, far from being preoccupied "with decisions made by individuals," is explicitly about how church communities might decide and the various roles played by different members in the community's decision process together. Fowl and Jones have a legitimate criticism when they complain that "community" is too little defined and described in the volume, though it is not treated as generically as they claim. The chapter on decision making makes this clear, among other places. Their criticism acknowledged, this present volume is an effort to give community a more extended, precise, and contextual meaning than *Bible and Ethics in the Christian Life* does.

and pioneering creativity through the practices integral to a visible way of life—are supplemented by a third: the community as haven or way station. The floundering of modernity and fragmentation of postmodernity mean that, curiously, we have come nearly full circle. Like a wrinkle in time we find ourselves, at the close of the second Christian millennium, not far from the terrain of Christians at the beginning of the first. Ours is also a "hellenistic" era—diverse, cosmopolitan, multilingual, -racial, -cultural,-religious, fragmented, eclectic, riddled by extremes of all kinds. Living in a dislocated world, people then felt and people now feel isolated or off center. Ours, too, is a time when the solidity of empire gives way and new configurations and alignments arise in different regions, often bedeviled by outbreaks of local violence. Those first Christians, like us, also worried about moral deformation everywhere, even as they rejoiced in the coming of a new world.

Many people living in such a time suffer from shaky structures, capricious policies and social practices, and plain fear. We reel from the sheer bewildering frenzy of such a world and wonder how to cope in both the short and long haul. We need sanctuaries, sacred spaces and places of safe retreat and balm very close to home, places of prayer, consolation, and the company of those who understand. We even resonate to the theme song that gathers the faithful at the bar in "Cheers": "Sometimes you want to go where everybody knows your name, and they're always glad you came. You wanna be where you can see everybody's troubles are all the same. You wanna go where everybody knows your name." This is the welcome of the sanctuary, the haven, the way station, what Bell Hooks refers to in a somewhat different context as "homeplace."[51]

The haven we have in view has a twist, however. It is the twist that comes from moving contrariwise to the usual function of religion in society. Generally religion functions in a socially conserving way, at least if the prominent groups in society have religious affiliations or, not having them, nonetheless appeal to them by way of the mayor's office or the famous "bully pulpit." This dynamic intensifies when a society fears instability, to say nothing of chaos. Religion is morally conservative as well, since the social function of religion is to supply transcendent sanc-

[51] Bell Hooks, *Yearning: Race, Gender, and Cultural Politics* (Boston: South End Press, 1990), 41ff.

tion for the dominant culture's way of life, or for dominant powers in the various subcommunities that inhabit a pluralist order.

Religion and morality classically function, then, as social glue, as a force for cultural cohesion. They bind and conserve. This explains why religiously underpinned conservatism is the expectation of many drawn to the churches or other religious communities, especially in troubled times. These communities are seen as places of solace and reassurance in a world of stress and strain. In short, they are havens, and havens by definition are places without convulsive change and conflict.

What is in view here, and proposed, is otherwise, at least in part. It is the church community as haven in the manner of many base Christian communities on the margins. These are havens for people who rather consistently experience "everything at once" and who know about world-weariness day in and day out. (World-weariness is increasing in our era—another parallel to the world in which Christianity was born and took fire.) They are havens of refreshment and of celebration around simple gifts. They are places of song, dance, and not a little silliness. They know how to do feasts, just as they know how to pray and be quiet and merciful to one another. They know how to resist the powers of death and make of their "homeplace communities" solid sites of resistance and reconstruction.[52] The people here are pastoral people present to one another in time of trouble and joy.

Moral conviction cannot be sustained—indeed, almost none of the dimensions of the moral life can be—without such havens and way stations. It is cruel and fruitless to call for social transformation in a long season of unavoidable experimentation without at the same time providing this community haven. The community of struggle should also be the community of mercy on the mountain.

Middle Americans need to hear another reason for the church as haven in the manner best known to communities of resistance. The long climb of modernity on the path of progress and the relative political stability for the bourgeoisie over most of a century in this nation has fostered its own illusion: the illusion that unity and harmony underlie

---

[52]Ibid., 41. It is important to say both resistance and reconstruction, since the skills needed for one are not the same as those for the other. For one account of this, see Charles Villa-Vicencio, *A Theology of Reconstruction: Nation-Building and Human Rights* (Cambridge: Cambridge University Press, 1992). We have assumed this in the discussion of pioneering creativity and practices.

civilization and social conflict is an irksome aberration rather than the standard condition of things, the normal condition Reinhold Niebuhr called "the endless cycle of social conflict."[53] Even more fundamentally, middle Americans have little sense that life is tragic, not given to predictability or control, and resistant to happy endings. This bourgeois innocence, together with assumed stability and harmony, expresses the basic tenet of modernity that steady improvement is possible, with no foreseeable end in view.[54] Although this is clearly utopian, and at odds with a Christian vision of history as tragic but graced, that does not loosen its grip on people who have experienced just enough good fortune to bolster such a view.

When the grip is forcibly loosened by hammerings of brute facts, however, and what was thought to be "natural" turns out to be but another historical chapter in an ever-changing tale, the metaphysically disappointed need a place for community pastoral care. They need the compassion of a haven whose own identity, rooted in history like an old cypress, knew all along that suffering and chaos, fear and uncertainty, even catastrophe, were as much the sinews of life and the occasions of faith as reliable friends and each year's sure turning. This is the way station that knows that not all the pieces of the puzzle of life can be found, that the ones found do not always fit, and that the picture formed isn't what was expected. This is the sanctuary that knows full well that life itself is cruciform and that Jesus has gone ahead of us on the journey, but not instead of us. This is also the sanctuary that knows there is water for the thirsty, salve for the weary, laughter for the needy, and forgiveness for fresh beginnings.

From another angle, this is haven as counterdrama to modernity's misplaced confidence and postmodernity's empty fragmentation. In a protracted period of fragments and the nonprogressive end of modernity's dream, so much depends on the right kind of fragments and the right kind of practices and other actions. Some fragments are fit only for the dustbin of history, Bonhoeffer wrote, while others, only completed by God, are in the manner of the fugue. "If our life is but the remotest reflection of such a fragment," he went on, "if we accumulate, at least for

---

[53]Niebuhr's *Moral Man and Immoral Society* (New York: Charles Scribner's Sons, 1932), as cited in Christopher Lasch, *The True and Only Heaven: Progress and Its Critics* (New York: W. W. Norton, 1991), 381. Lasch does not provide the page number.
[54]Ibid., 47.

a short time, a wealth of themes and weld them into a harmony in which the great counterpoint is maintained from start to finish . . . we will not bemoan the fragmentariness of our life, but rather rejoice in it."[55]

Yet rejoicing in the fragments requires a havenplace, a cell of renewal that washes all in the purifying waters of gratitude and contrition, a place that fosters courage and accommodates risk and venturing responsibility. "We have learned, rather too late, that action comes, not from thought, but from a readiness for responsibility," Bonhoeffer wrote on the occasion of the baptism of his grandnephew. "For you, thought and action will enter on a new relationship: your thinking will be confined to your responsibilities in action. With us thought was often the luxury of the onlooker; with you it will be entirely subordinated to action."[56] Reflecting the bourgeois world that first nurtured him, then fell apart, Bonhoeffer went on to say: "We thought we could make our way in life with reason and justice, and when both failed, we felt that we were at the end of our tether. We have constantly exaggerated the importance of reason and justice in the course of history."[57] So the task, it turns out, is that we "shall have to keep our lives rather than shape them, to hope rather than plan, to hold out rather than march forward."[58]

All these disjunctions, which Bonhoeffer experienced long before middle Americans, only served to deepen and radicalize his cell-and-movement understanding of church in a time of "no ground under our feet."[59] "Our earlier words are . . . bound to lose their force and cease," he concluded, "and our being Christians today will be limited to two things: prayer and righteous action. . . . All Christian thinking, speaking, and organizing must be born anew out of this prayer and action."[60] "Prayer" is shorthand for the community as haven, as way station; "righteous action" is shorthand for its practices and its actions, undertaken with others inside and outside the church, with a view toward responsibility in history for the sake of coming generations. For a season of fragments and uncertainty, more than this vital spiritual refuge with a social

---

[55]Dietrich Bonhoeffer, "23 February 1944," in *Letters and Papers from Prison*, ed. Eberhard Bethge, enlarged ed. (New York: Macmillan, 1972), 219.
[56]Ibid., "Thoughts on the Day of the Baptism of Dietrich Wilhelm Ruediger Bethge," 298.
[57]Ibid.
[58]Ibid., 297.
[59]The title of a subsection in the essay "After Ten Years," ibid., 3.
[60]Ibid., 300.

consciousness and community bonds is not asked, nor required. It is tuned to living with ambiguity, messiness, and disappointment.

The last role of the church as a servant community of the moral life is the role of moral critic. This is perhaps the most threatening and most unsettling, because Christian freedom stands off to the side on independent grounds not easily intimidated. "Armies can be defeated," one commentator puts it. "With martyrs, it's a different matter."[61]

I frequently cite Monica Hellwig in support of this critical freedom, with her simple line that "Jesus lived as though God reigned and none else had any power over him."[62] So did, so should, and so does the faith community. Thus did those first people of the way, at least on their better days. They were ordinary folk, a fact that astonished even someone as accustomed to dramatic surprises as Paul (see 1 Cor. 1:26-30). But living as though God reigns and none else has power means a thorough critique of this present age, at the heart of which so often are conflicts with "principalities and powers."

This kind of moral criticism, then, is a public stance that relativizes all other authorities. That in turn peels moral legitimation from the present cultural patterns and social forms. Granted, they may, upon discerning inspection, still be appropriate and valid, but now only proximately and provisionally so, a status no one in power seems much to appreciate, ourselves included. Accepted family patterns, the going economic and political arrangements of systems, current community polities, and, not least, the standard ordering of ideas and perspectives themselves (ideology) are all moved from the status of practical necessity to that of review and possibility. No particular arrangements are categorically indispensable, nor are any categorically forbidden. Jesus means a radical freedom, to recall Paul again. When social forms build up community and world, conserve them. When not, change them. The forms for life together are as open-ended as the imaginations and the resources of those struggling to live "as though God now reigned and none else had power."[63] Here is full Christian freedom for moral critique and con-

---

[61]M. J. Akbar, "At the Center of the World," *New York Times*, 10 January 1992, A29. Akbar was writing about Islamic fundamentalists and not Christians. His characterization nonetheless fits precisely much of what we know of early Christian martyrs.

[62]Monica Hellwig, *Jesus: The Compassion of God* (Wilmington, Del.: Michael Glazier, 1965), 81.

[63]My discussion of these three roles is adapted from an earlier writing, "The

struction, the feisty freedom that Luther claimed made the Christian both lord of all and subject to none, yet servant of all subject to all.[64]

The constructive side of this critical freedom is empowerment or, differently said, active moral agency. In his Nobel Peace Prize acceptance speech, Martin Luther King, Jr., claimed that the most important feature of the civil rights movement was the "direct participation of masses in protest, rather than reliance on indirect methods which frequently do not involve masses in action at all."[65] It was later confirmation of what he had already witnessed in the Montgomery bus boycott: "a once fear-ridden people had been transformed"[66] by community participation driven by a courageous freedom that would not be turned back by fire hoses, dogs, and a phalanx of unjust laws, customs, and institutions several centuries deep.

This is perhaps the place to bring this book to a close,[67] since moral critique nicely returns us to the opening chapter—namely, with the contention that moral discernment and judgment are inescapable tasks of a proper community of moral conviction. This includes moral judgment of the community's own moral patterns and choices, including the practices of its way. It also ranges beyond self-critique and takes in, at least

---

Public Vocation of an Eschatological Community," *Union Seminary Quarterly Review* 42, 4 (1988): 28–31.

[64]See Martin Luther, "The Freedom of a Christian," available, among other places, in Martin Luther, *Three Treatises* (Philadelphia: Muhlenberg Press, 1960), 262–316.

[65]King as cited by Lasch, *The True and Only Heaven*, 404. King's chief writings, including the Nobel Prize acceptance speech, are available in James M. Washington, ed., *A Testament of Hope: The Essential Writings of Martin Luther King, Jr.* (San Francisco: Harper & Row, 1986).

[66]King, as cited by Lasch, ibid., 405.

[67]A helpful article for this discussion, but too late to be assimilated, is Thomas W. Ogletree, "The Public Witness of the Christian Churches," *The Annual of the Society of Christian Ethics 1992* (Washington, D.C.: Georgetown University Press, 1992), 43–74. While I agree with much, I judge the *problématique humaine* of the day as more problematic than he does. I am less confident of the viability of the present civilizational framework and more convinced that Bonhoeffer's picture of fragmentation and a long season of experimentation is correct. This gives my portrayal of the churches as moral communities more "sectarian" tones than Ogletree's. Neither of us is sectarian in the stereotypical sense, however, since we are both concerned to affirm the public presence and responsibility of the churches, as well as the necessity of the churches to learn from the world.

theoretically, God's entire world. And it returns us to the opening chapter's confidence that our times call for a religious community's moral gifts and staying power despite its checkered, sometimes horrendous, history.

What remains to be said about the four roles is only that they, like the life of the community itself, come together focally in worship. Worship for a people of the way was and is "the communal cultivation of an alternative construction of society and of history."[68] In a long season of necessary social experimention, exactly that is needed. "An alternative construction of society and history" is, in fact, the reply to Paz's opening call for renewed community as the means for renewed society. But wholly apart from the circumstantial usefulness of such community, naming and praising God in worship is the first reason for the community's being. It does not exist for its own sake but for the neighbor's and to praise God and enjoy God forever.[69]

While well aware of the inadequacy Tom Wingo reminded us of at the outset—that "the only word for goodness is goodness, and it is not enough"—I have sought to revive for our time and place, and especially for the muddled middle of the public church, the early, practices-centered, community-centered metaphor for the Christian life as the life of the people of the way. That which brings community to life is, by another name, also the experience of God among us. It has a special fit for the season and place we live, a servant kind of fit appropriate to the church as a community of moral formation and conviction. And it has the deepest possible resonance with the formative beginnings of the Christian moral life in the God-intoxicated Jesus and his community of ordinary, hesitant, emboldened people. It is faithful and practical in the same moment and dares to live the conviction that the journey is home, and home for good.

---

[68]John Howard Yoder, *The Priestly Kingdom* (Notre Dame: University of Notre Dame Press, 1984), 43.

[69]Even though this chapter has used Christian symbols, allusions, and theological themes throughout, it has only begun to spell out what Christian traditions and current ferment might mean for the content and shape of Christian community. There are numerous works which do so, among them Paul D. Hanson, *The People Called: The Growth of Community in the Bible* (San Francisco: Harper San Francisco, 1986) and Bruce C. Birch, *Let Justice Roll Down: The Old Testament, Ethics, and Christian Life* (Louisville: Westminster/John Knox Press, 1991).

Index